Colleen Connaughton
Monique Elise
Ryan Hampton
Jessica Lopez

The Addiction Diaries

STORIES OF DARKNESS, HOPE
AND ALL THAT FALLS IN BETWEEN.

EDITED BY ANNA DAVID

Jennifer Lovely
Jacq Maren
Victoria English Martin
Paul Roux
Lauren Schwarzfeld

Among Others

Launch Pad Publishing
www.launchpadpub.com

ISBN-13: 978-1-951407-27-8
ISBN-13: 978-1-951407-26-1 (ebook)

To get more information about the book and its contributors, scan the QR code below.

Contents

Introduction

I'm writing this while the world is in the midst of a pandemic.

But there's another pandemic that started its attacks long before we knew that Corona was anything more than a beer. It's called addiction—and it takes the lives of more than 67,000 people a year—in addition to the roughly 88,000 who die of alcohol-related causes every year.

Because of those numbers, and because addiction is a disease that impacts all races, cultures and socioeconomic levels—taking down people from Park Avenue to park benches—putting together a book called *The Addiction Diaries* was a fairly audacious idea.

I've been sober nearly 20 years and have written a number of books and dozens of articles on the topic. This means that I knew enough to ask myself: How could we possibly tell the stories of the wide swath of people who have been impacted?

I'll admit that upon original conception, I wasn't sure we could. And while I'm not saying that we've included every story possible (that would be impossible), the tales these authors tell here are tragic, inspiring, heartbreaking, illuminating—and perhaps most importantly, all unique.

Whether it's a concerned sister trying to carry out her mother's dying wish to save her gambling-addicted brother, a former bank robber reflecting on his nearly two decades of sobriety, a daughter hearing her abusive mom admit her mistakes decades later or a former heroin addict who first attempted suicide at 12 finding a calm life, you'll find yourself astounded by these stories that display the strength and ultimate triumph of the human spirit.

There are also stories from a mom who realized she needed to break the cycle of functional alcoholism, a Filipina woman who learned to break free of violence in jail, a South African man who found sobriety while feeding pigs on a farm, a mom who discovered that she could withstand the societal pressures of the #winemoms, a recovery advocate who hid his sexuality until he was ready to come out and a mother of two incarcerated addicts who watched them suffer through horror after horror before they found sobriety.

And that's just the beginning.

In short, this collection of essays demonstrates the profound impact addiction has on people from all socioeconomic levels, races, sexual identifications and beliefs—as well as the fact that recovery is possible in even the most hopeless situations.

If you're familiar with recovery, you'll recognize a number of the thoughts, feelings and actions these writers describe. If addiction is a new topic for you, you'll come to understand it in ways you never could before. Either way, I imagine you'll find yourself astounded by the courage, wisdom and strength of these contributors.

Their lives will linger with you long after you read about them.

Anna David, September 2020

Home Sweet Heroin

Monique Elise

I'm alive today because death didn't want me. It wasn't for a lack of trying. By all rights, I should have died long ago. But here I am, bundled on my deck with a hot cup of coffee and a cozy blanket, looking out into nature. It's more than looking, though; it's savoring the tranquility within. It's feeling happy to be alive—grateful, even. I feel it now, on my deck, looking at the rows of towering Douglas firs. It's like they are shielding and protecting me inside a warm, safe haven.

But it wasn't always this way.

My childhood was chaotic. My mother was a wild and adrenaline-seeking kid when she had me at 16. She did her best. I can only imagine how terrified and traumatized she must have been after the death of my biological dad. He died two months before I was born while drinking and driving. She found new dads for me, but I don't think she loved herself enough to choose the healthy ones. The men she loved carried deep wounds and hurts that led to addictions as well as physical, sexual and emotional pain against our family. But even in the midst of chaos, addiction and abuse, my mother managed to go to school, get her GED and even become a social worker who helped at-risk youth. But that didn't last. How could it?

———

I woke up one morning and there was my new stepdad. I was 11. I had met him once before on the street, randomly; he recognized me as my mother's child and gave me a candy bar. I didn't know they were dating until the morning he was in my house. They were in love and on drugs. They were up all night and slept all day and you didn't dare wake them. That's the year things went from bad to worse.

My previous stepdad was gone by then. The day before, he had been pacing back and forth in their smoke-filled bedroom, listening through a baby monitor to my mom and her new guy having sex in the garage. He swallowed bottles of Budweiser and sucked on a string of cigarettes, alternating between fits of rage and down-on-his-knees despair. Later that night, he stole my babysitting money, stuffed it into my school backpack and disappeared for years.

I was a good kid growing up, not only living with my mom and stepdads but also with my grandma, younger brother and two younger sisters. I enjoyed school—my escape from the chaos at home.

But by the time I was 12, that all changed.

I didn't want to be at home and I didn't want to be at school.

So I hitchhiked to escape.

The first time was when I was 12. Instead of going home after school, I hitchhiked to Calgary with my friend Kelly and her boyfriend, David. We didn't care where we were going and Calgary just happened to be where our driver was headed. When we needed a place to sleep at night, we broke into a camper or slept outside of store-fronts. David had stolen meth from his dad and we snorted that. It was my first time using hard drugs.

I didn't really like how meth made me feel but I had this attitude that I would try anything once. I didn't care what happened to me. I kept hitchhiking and doing drugs. In some ways, I almost hoped that I would die. I had this fantasy of being with my dad in the sky.

Days later, I acted on this feeling: barefoot, arms outstretched like Jesus to the cross, robe wide open—my 12-year-old body naked and exposed. Resembling the girl from *The Exorcist*, I sprinted toward oncoming traffic in a violent rage. "Hit me!" I screamed. "Just kill me!"

I blinked. Nothing. Fast-moving vehicles swerved around me. I dropped hard to my knees, listening to the wailing horns fly past me.

By 14, I was hitchhiking regularly and sleeping in the streets—always wondering if this would be the time my 92-pound body would be flung into the ditch. It's not that I was actively seeking to be strangled to death—more that I was okay if it happened.

It wasn't long before I wrote goodbye letters, chopped off all my hair and swallowed two bottles of pills. Days later, I woke up with feeding tubes in my nose, unable to open eyes that felt heavy—as if my eyelids had been stitched shut. A nurse held my hand and told me that I was lucky to be alive and that someone was looking out for me. I knew it was my dad.

But then, when I was 15, I met heroin and I no longer wanted to die. Heroin wrapped me in a warm, heated blanket of euphoria. It loved me with blissful eyeballs-rolling-back intensity—a love that coursed through me with warm pulsating explosions.

The first time I tried heroin, I was with my brother and my boyfriend, John. We had stolen the heroin from my mom. I thought as long as I wasn't prostituting myself or using needles, I was okay. Those were the only two criteria.

But over the next several years, our family addiction to heroin worsened. My grandma and two little sisters watched as my mom, stepdad, brother and I spiraled. We dragged them into a nightmare. Police raids were common, as was an eviction almost every three months. Heat and hot water became scarce. There was never any food. If they were lucky, I'd remember to steal them something to eat. My malnourished grandma with her degenerating mind would smile meekly and thank me. But my guilt was quickly replaced by a desperate hunger for heroin. So I'd stand on the corner and pretend to be a prostitute. Because I robbed the johns instead of selling my body, I thought I was okay. I wasn't an addict yet.

The worst thing, though, is that heroin stopped working. It stopped loving me. There was no more happiness—just loss and despair. I felt it most fiercely after my sisters were removed and placed in foster care.

———

A couple of months after my sisters were taken, I woke up to an eerie voice methodically speaking to me from the television: "Who you associate with determines the outcome of your life." These words flung me upright in bed. I looked around. I was with my mom and some random man in his apartment at the Rafter G Hotel. We were all on heroin. I scanned the room and saw the crack pipe, needles—the whole train wreck of our lives—and had a forceful urge to get out of there. I ran.

The urge to run lingered in my bones for days until an unlikely man knocked on my door. It was Mike. It had been three years since I'd last seen him, when I was 15 and he'd punched me in the face, knocking me out of a moving boat. Today, he was looking for my roommate, who had stolen his truck.

I expected anger, but instead, he looked at me with concern from behind his thick, 1970s aviator glasses.

"I heard you're pretty fucked up," he said. "I find it really sad. I thought of all the people, you would be the one to get out of here."

He gestured inside and asked if he could come in and talk. I led him into my living room and sat across from him on a white plastic stool. We sat in silence a moment, as he lit us both cigarettes.

Mike inhaled. "I've always felt bad for you. You don't seem to have anyone looking out for you."

His words wafted from his mouth in a cloud of smoke and punched me in the chest. It wasn't that I didn't already know, but hearing it said out loud physically hurt.

"If I gave you an opportunity to get out," he asked, "would you take it?"

I told him I planned on getting out. He smiled. "Well, I'm actually looking for someone to run a grow-op for me in Vancouver. I could set you up, but you have to be clean. You cannot be on heroin. And you cannot tell anyone where you're going. That's the exchange."

I left with him. In some ways, I was shocked that I would leave with a 40-year-old man who had already been violent with me—and not tell a soul where I was going. But I knew this was a lifeline and it was my only chance.

And so, just like that, I was in Vancouver, five hours

from home, alone and sick. I wasn't the only one alone, though—our family had been decimated. Each of us split off, like branches broken from a tree—my brother and stepdad in jail, my sisters in foster care, Mom floundering God knows where and Grandma at home grasping to the remains of her fractured mind. There was nothing I could do but get myself out.

So I stayed in Vancouver. And over the next several months, I used prescription opioids and methadone to slowly wean myself off of heroin. Within one year, I stopped taking all opioids. At the grow-op, Mike introduced me to Ryan, who was the only person with whom I was allowed to have contact. He talked to me about what I was doing with my life. And over time, he taught me how to enter society with life skills—such as how to drive a car instead of hitchhiking and how to create a resume to get a legal job. He convinced me to go back to school and leave the grow operation.

He gave me the tools to create a new life.

In the end, as unorthodox as it was, my experience running the grow-op led to success getting clean since it provided me with what I needed while I was in transition. I had housing and food, but most importantly, I had a job—a sense of purpose: thirsty plants in need of my attention and care. Having my basic needs met provided a foundation to build a new life.

It felt like I had entered a new world, a different dimension altogether. It was a steep climb from where I had circled down into hell and lived beneath the people who bustled to and from work. The air had been different there—thick and heavy, weighing a thousand pounds. The color was different there, too: perpetually overcast and darkened by shades of bleak, grey sadness.

But in this new world, my life changed color. And in

time I built a real estate business and became a home-owner and landlord. I cultivated positive friendships and improved my relationships with my family, including my mother, who has also been off heroin and crack since 2010. Today, my wild and adrenaline-seeking mother finds joy in running, dragon boating and building new memories with her family.

Not all of my family made it out. Some died and some are still strung out. But I still strive to break the long family legacy of addiction for my sisters and nephews by modeling a new life. In the end, just as that eerie voice had once warned, the people I chose to associate with helped to shape the outcome of my life. And I hope to do the same.

Today, I'm happy death didn't want me. I'm happy to be alive, even though it's been a long journey—one that's not yet over. For years, I built my life on the surface with a career and homes, but those old wounds and ghosts that led me to heroin addiction and suicidal feelings were still there, lying dormant beneath the surface.

I would soon learn that healing happens in stages. I wasn't out of the clear. But luckily, our bodies know when it's safe from imminent danger, and show us what we need to see. What we need to feel. And what we need to heal.

Going forward, I want to help others cultivate the calm life that I experience today—a life I no longer try to escape. I'm building an online platform for women to heal their trauma and addictions. It's a nonjudgmental space where women can dive into the dark and gritty parts of life. It's my hope that by sharing our stories, we can all heal, transform our lives and create profound change.

Quit Your Quitting

Bucky Sinister

I'm a quitter. I've quit jobs, relationships, schools, cities, meals, sports, hobbies, parties and concerts. I switched majors from engineering to art to film to creative writing and went to three schools. I give movies 20 minutes to hook me. Books get a chapter to stay open. From 1984 to 1989, I lived in Arkansas, Boston, St. Louis, Los Angeles and San Francisco. The great irony is the only thing I should have quit I held on to loyally: drinking.

I started drinking senior year of high school. Drug phases came and went, but the alcohol was always there. I chose drinking over several careers, my relationship with my family and the best girlfriends I had. I lived in horrible places and hung out with terrible people. It took the unnecessary death of a roommate to get me to finally try putting the bottle down for good. I quit drinking at 32 years old.

I felt like quitting 12-step recovery as well. So much of it bothered me. The literature was poorly written. There were many conflicting statements about policy and tradition. Most of all, I didn't want to go to churches and hear anyone talk about prayer and God. But I was determined to stick with it and told myself I could only quit if I found a different method of recovery. I've been in it now since 2002.

Over the course of working my fourth step and fifth steps, then having to go back and do them over again, I found out my heaviest resentments were for people who had what I wanted, and it came down to pursuits I gave up on. If I quit something, and you didn't, well fuck you then. You don't deserve it. You had it handed to you, you were given a break I didn't have or your parents gave it to you. I felt as if I had been cheated, when the reality is that most often, I had walked away when things were difficult. Not only that, but I carried strong dislike for anyone who had accomplished more than me. This was the source of a lot of chronic depression and frustration for me.

I created a separate inventory of everything I quit in life. The list was stunning. It was easy to see the negative long-term impact of all this. I tended to quit right before a commitment, a graduation or a promotion. I was always afraid of that next step. I was trying to keep my life wherever it was at the time. Sadly, I never appreciated where I was. I said I wanted that next step, but I bailed out before I was about to move on.

My amends for this was to figure out what I could still complete. It was too late to rejoin the junior high basketball team, and there was no way I was moving back to Arkansas. There were two things on the list that I could try: my college degree and standup comedy. My college degree came first. It took three years to get my BA at 35.

———

Back when I turned 21, I went down to The Holy City Zoo and signed up on their open mic list. The Zoo is a legendary tiny bar in San Francisco that was the playground of local greats like Dana Carvey and Robin Williams. I went up without preparing and I sucked. I walked away thinking I was really bad at it and didn't try again.

At the time, I was doing really well in the poetry and performance art world. I was giving readings at crowded nightclubs and holding my own against other performers who were twice my age. South of Market, I had to wait outside the clubs until my name was called, then run in and do my set. I would go backstage, snort a line of meth, finish someone's drink and then have to leave into the night. I loved it. I thought, *Well, I'm good at poetry but I suck at comedy.*

Through random chance, in 1992, I met Patton Oswalt and Blaine Capatch. We all hung out at a café on Haight Street called The Horseshoe. They were the funniest guys in the place. When I got to know them, they told me they had moved to San Francisco to become comedians. *Good luck with that,* I sarcastically thought to myself. But they were so good! I started seeing them around town and met a lot of the other local comics. Eventually, after working their way up, they moved to LA and started writing for the first season of *MAD TV*.

About four years later, I went to Cobb's Comedy Club to watch them open for Rick Overton. They were good before, but now, they were tearing the place up. They were on a whole different level. They did improv scenes with Rick and it looked like the most fun you could have on stage.

I wish I could do that, I thought. *But I'm 26. I'm way too old to start that now. You have to start when you're younger.*

But really, it was the fear of not being able to do it. The one singular trauma of the one bad open mic and the self-defeating voice of the alcoholic that kept me from trying again.

Years passed and Patton kept improving his career. There were specials and CDs. He was a recurring character on a sitcom. He got weird movie roles that played right into his sensibility. I followed his work like I used to follow bands from their first gig to their first records.

One night, I watched him from backstage at a sold out 400-person room that was one show of five like it that weekend. He was so good. Most of all he was having fun. The performance art scene was literally gone by then, and I wasn't having fun on the poetry scene anymore; there was a whole new style and sensibility that didn't fit with my work.

I wish I could do that, I thought. *But I'm 37. I'm way too old to start that now. You have to start when you're younger.*

It struck me that had I started when I first thought that same thing 10 years earlier, I would be good enough to be opening for him rather than just watching from backstage.

My sponsor had a fun time with the decision. There's nothing they like more than assigning inventories. I had to create fear inventories, expectation lists and a regular 10th-step-type assessment of shows I went to and people with whom I interacted.

When anyone in the industry sees a 37-year-old comic, they assume the comic has been at it for 17 years. I was as good as a 20-year-old comic and no one had heard of me. It's like being a 40-year-old virgin. There's nothing wrong with it, but people definitely think it's unusual.

All I control is how hard I work at it; I can't control what people think of me. This has been the hardest lesson in my creative life. Trying to control other people's opinions of my work and the work of others put me in bad places, and I used it as an excuse to drink. I saw myself as a misunderstood genius, the victim of some literary critic's crimes. I was focused on how I was seen rather than my own effort.

I've never gotten far, career-wise, in standup. I've gotten paid work in comedy clubs and opened for a few of my favorite comics. I ended up with a couple of tiny film roles after people saw me on stage. I had a great time producing my own live show for over 10 years. But career goals aren't anything more than an idea of where you're going.

I've moved from a "What I Had" perspective to a "What's Next?" perspective. I look forward in life rather than backward. As a creative person, I must enjoy the journey of creation instead of relying on the reception of the audience. Any time an old feeling pops up, an old regret of something I should have done, I immediately go into a mode of "What can I do right now?" I determine how the negative experience can help me move forward.

I don't know what comedy holds for me. I don't know if I'll break through to another level. But the process of chasing it gave me the life tools I needed to get through other new experiences, jobs and relationships. I may eventually quit comedy as well, but if I do, it will be out of love for myself rather than fear.

Breaking the Cycle

Jessica Lopez

My parents couldn't have been more different. My mom was emotionally present and very involved. She never made me feel like a burden. She never drank too much. She was the glue that kept our family together.

My dad, on the other hand, made me feel like a burden all the time. Anything having to do with emotions was not his forte.

"You're too sensitive," he'd say.

Every night, he drank his two to three glasses of gin religiously. I don't think the alcohol was the only thing that caused him to be so removed, but I don't think it helped him to be more connected either. Looking back, he might have been struggling with mental illness and self-medicating with alcohol. He seemed to be unhappy and easily irritated much of the time. Nothing pleased him. Was he depressed? Was he dealing with anxiety?

When I hit my teen years and my brother left for college, my dad grew even more distant and unhappy. Though his father was a non-drinker and his mother only a social drinker, his parents always emphasized the importance of how you looked on the outside rather than dealing with the "negative" emotions on the inside, so he was just behaving in the way he'd learned to behave. He lived robotically—get up, go to work, come home, have a drink, eat dinner, watch TV, go to bed, repeat.

It would take me a while to realize I had grown up in a household with a functioning alcoholic, because functional alcoholism is sly. It can look like normal drinking. Many people's conception of an alcoholic is someone who's sloppy, falling over in the street and not functioning at all. If you're showing up to work every day, as my dad was, many people assume you don't have a problem.

The other issue with functional alcoholism, besides the fact that it can be hard to recognize, is the quiet damage done to the people around the alcoholic, particularly their kids. I craved my dad's attention and affection and not getting those things left a hole in my heart.

———

Since drinking was so normalized in my childhood, it only made sense for me to start experimenting early.

My parents always kept liquor in the cabinet. At 13, I thought, *I'll try a little bit of vodka. They won't notice.* I didn't get drunk at first. I just took little swigs here and there.

By 16, I was drinking heavily, mostly at parties with my friends. I had a very high tolerance for alcohol. Even when I was wasted, swerving in and out of blackouts, people couldn't necessarily tell that I was drunk.

Alcohol helped me be more outgoing. I became the life of the party. My anxiety faded to background noise, my pain was numbed. From the ages of 15 to 20, I was stuck in an abusive relationship. Drinking heavily helped me ignore the voice inside that was saying, *You need to get out of this and take care of yourself.*

I continued to pour alcohol on that voice until one morning that changed my life.

After a night of hard drinking, I woke up shaking uncontrollably. A few people, my so-called friends at the time, told me to just drink more; that would make the shakes go away. So I drank more and it worked, but this experience stayed with me. I knew waking up with the shakes was serious. Had I become dependent on alcohol?

I was so scared that at the age of 20, I quit drinking. I also found the strength and courage to leave my abuser. Shortly thereafter, I met my husband, who was and still is my biggest supporter.

———

In my mid-20's, my dad's drinking became more of an issue. He tried to quit several times but would always go back. Although I never saw him drink more than his usual two to three glasses of gin a night, I started to suspect he was drinking in secret. He'd come home at six and an hour later, be passed out in his chair in the living room. It didn't add up.

At one point, after having announced again that he'd quit drinking, he came up from the basement with a glass of gin in his hand. My mom and I later found an empty bottle hidden inside his workbench. Eventually, he explained that he'd put it there hoping that the inconvenient walk down to the basement would deter him from drinking. Clearly, he was struggling and he knew that. I never told my dad I was worried about his drinking, because we didn't have that type of open dialogue. Maybe I didn't expect that he would hear me.

Amazingly, toward the end of his life, my dad did quit drinking. I still have no idea what finally inspired him to stop. He lost weight. He was doing well. He'd started biking to work and in general, he seemed happier. Our relationship was beginning to heal. On my birthday, he brought me a dozen pink flowers and a chocolate advent calendar. Normally, I got gifts my mom had purchased signed, "Love, Mom and Dad." I was awestruck by my dad's gesture, and also holding my breath. Would it last?

Close to two months after my birthday, my dad was diagnosed with liver cancer. Even though he was a functional alcoholic all his life, and even though he'd finally made the brave choice to quit, he couldn't change the past. All those years of abuse had unfortunately caught up with him.

My dad died the way he had lived. He was emotionally unattached about the diagnosis and in denial about his fate. He did, however, acknowledge the reality once. He came to my room and said, "I really fucked up."

"Dad," I said, "it's okay."

I spent the 12 weeks leading up to his death caring for him. Regardless of our relationship, he was my father. I put my emotions aside and loved him in the way I'd always wanted him to love me. I had to make hard decisions. I took his car keys away because he was too sick to drive. I spent the last night of his life helping him rotate between morphine and Lorazepam every 45 minutes to keep him comfortable until he passed early in the morning. He was only 60 and I was 27. Watching someone you love pass away is difficult, and when you have a strained relationship with that person, it's even harder. There were so many things still left unsaid when my dad died, and so many wounds left unhealed.

———

I still don't understand my dad's behavior, but I have found forgiveness. I know that he did the best he could do with the tools he was given.

I also know that alcoholism is a disease and not a moral failing. Whether the alcoholic is functional or not, the consequences are devastating for both the alcoholic and everyone around them. Since my dad's death, I've lost an aunt (my dad's sister) and an uncle (my mom's brother) to alcohol-related diseases and accidents.

I often wonder how many of the alcoholics on both sides of my family suffered from mental illness and were drinking to self-medicate. I know when I was drinking, that's exactly what I was doing: numbing the pain by drowning it out.

I still suffer from anxiety. I also have PTSD from the abusive relationship I left when I was 20. Over the years, I've learned ways to treat my symptoms that don't involve medicating myself with substances. I've chosen various modes of therapy to heal myself and to change the pattern going forward with my own children. My goal is to leave them with a different legacy than the one that was offered to me by my father.

In our house, my kids aren't exposed to a lot of drinking, so they understand that alcohol isn't a necessary part of life. I try to be present with them and to allow them to express themselves. I want them to feel safe and protected and never like a burden. I try to give them everything that my dad wasn't able to give to me. I want to show them what self-care looks like and that it is not selfish. I want our household to be a place where mental health is just as much a priority as physical health. My hope is that by allowing my kids the space to share their feelings now, they won't want to self-medicate down the road.

The pain of having a functioning alcoholic parent is confusing and corrosive. Because if it didn't look that bad, if your parent wasn't out in the street or losing jobs or hurting you physically, then how bad was it, really? Did it really affect you?

Recently, I was telling a friend about my dad and she said, "Wow, my dad was totally a functional alcoholic, too, but I never thought about it that way."

Functional alcoholism is more prevalent than we know, and in my opinion, it's not discussed often enough. I want to give a voice to the children of functioning alcoholics who feel confused, abandoned and ashamed. I want them to know just because their parents went to work and did all the things that society deems important, that doesn't mean their alcoholism didn't cause pain. I want people who grew up in the same type of environment as I did to feel validated, and to know that it's possible to heal.

The Dive Bar Bus Tour

Emerson Dameron

I have two main drives in my life—a longing for human connection and a desperate desire to be left alone. So I try to connect with people in ways that are pretty much guaranteed to fail.

It's several years before I stopped drinking. I've recently moved to Los Angeles, a metro area of 12 million souls, and I'm having a hard time making friends. So I go online to meetup.com, as is the custom of the time, and find some groups that seem to be aligned with my interests.

There's the Los Angeles Drinking Society, Safari Barflies and Dive Bar Adventures, which is promoting its annual flagship event, the Dockweiler Beach Party and Dive Bar Bus Tour. They're hustling the ticket sales, because in order to pay for the bus that's required, they have to sell a lot of tickets. I say, *This seems like a good way to round out the summer*. And I sign up.

I ride down on the 110. I ride over on the 105. I'm getting pumped. I'm listening to high-energy hip hop. I'm going to make some new friends. I'm going to have a good time.

In the early afternoon, I arrive at Dockweiler Beach, LA's designated party beach, known for its burning bonfires, biohazard bathrooms and affable gangbangers. The event has a beach party theme, so I've got on a floral pattern. Looking good, feeling good.

I see the Dive Bar Adventures contingent. They've got fuzzy hats. They've got flashing lapel pins. And right away, I think, *I've made a mistake. This is too much.*

But I'm here now, so I start milling around. There's a guy with long, stringy hair who looks like he was kicked out of Mötley Crüe in its very early days, for good reason. He's screaming. I decide to give this man a wide berth. I don't want to get involved with his world.

There are some clusters of people who seem to already know each other. I introduce myself, surprised to find myself feeling intimidated before they've said anything. I've spent too much time alone lately. I thought I'd grow out of this. They seem cool and friendly, which makes me want to impress them. I'm not sure I have anything interesting to say, so I move along, hobbled by social awkwardness, eager to self-medicate.

I take a swig of the cherry red punch, mixed especially for this event, which tastes like cough syrup, turpentine and concussions. I feel a rush of blurry energy and a reassuring hug from the inside. I also feel myself getting a sunburn. I could have worn sunscreen, but I went in unprotected, because I want to feel the full experience. This is all about getting stupid. That's close enough to being happy.

I pick up some sand and let it run through my fingers, which is a sensation that comforted me as a child.

I see some people getting ready to get on the bus for the Dive Bar Bus Tour portion of the event. I get in line with them. This is something to do. I need something to do.

The bus rolls out to explore four of the South Bay's finest dive bars. Everyone on the bus is screaming. I notice I'm screaming. We have something in common. The soundtrack is '80s music played at ear-splitting volume, entirely midrange.

We get to Mo's Place, which is allegedly the inspiration for Moe's Tavern on *The Simpsons*. It's known for its cruel and neglectful customer service, which, as the adult child of alcoholics, makes me feel right at home.

Because it's taking a while to get a drink, I decide to make a new friend. I start talking to a young lady with dark hair and sad eyes who seems like she could use a friend, too. It goes the way things usually go when two lonely, awkward people try to connect but neither is really bringing it in the way it needs to be brought.

"Having fun?"

"Yeah."

"It's loud."

"Sure."

"There are a lot of people here."

"We're here, too."

I realize I need some extra charm. So I drink some of the punch that someone has smuggled inside in a Thermos. As I gulp, I feel myself hitting the mysterious zone known as The Glow, that interval in a drinking session in which everything works, everything is flowing, everything is illuminated, I light up like a jack-o-lantern, I'm charming, I like people, I like being around people and I like myself.

I stay in The Glow for about nine seconds before I go over the border, into the zone in which I behave like a stroke patient.

The bus rolls up to The Office in Downtown El Segundo. It serves "breakfast shots" with strips of bacon soaking in Early Times. I sit next to the screaming rock-and-roll guy. We become fast friends.

"I'm a piece of garbage."

"Some of my best friends are pieces of garbage."

I have now alienated the person I wanted to befriend and befriended the person I wanted to avoid. At this point, I'm just making sounds of approval or disapproval. Totally content-free. Which, if you pay attention, is actually how most conversation is. It's just more exaggerated when you're wasted.

"Yes!"

"Hell yeah."

"No!"

"I'm not going to argue with you, man, I'm not part of your world."

Clink.

In the dark of Ercoles in Manhattan Beach, I give up on meaningfully connecting with anyone. *Y'all aren't on my level. I'm not part of your world.*

I float from group to group, quipping and ranting incoherently. In my mind, I've become a country singer, or Bukowski, an idiot savant character, a dispenser of shocking and moving bon mots, who breaks open your heart and then evaporates. I'm a two-dimensional illusion, unencumbered by the three-dimensional aggravations and indignities of humanity, adulthood or continuity. I'm an artist. I'm magic. The party is where I am. You're invited, but you probably can't get in.

"Are you okay?" asks the bouncer, looking unsympathetic.

"I'm good. I'm here. I'm doing my best. It's the best I can do."

"Stay with your group, all right?"

The trip ends at Baja Sharkeez in Hermosa Beach. I

flag down a waitress who's sexy in a focus-grouped way. I receive the Jello Shot Injection, a jello shot delivered through a plastic novelty syringe. As the sugary slime runs down my throat, I realize I have crossed a threshold. I am 100% gone. I am banjoed, pixelated, blackout drunk.

Surrendering all of my faculties to oblivion puts me in a position in which I'm required to trust people. My fellow Dive Bar Adventurers help me get back to Dockweiler Beach. I'm heedless, anesthetized, a drooling radish of a man, but still part of their world. I will acknowledge their kindness in my four-star review.

Back at the beach, the party rages on. There are few more hours until sundown. The punch keeps flowing. People are still going strong.

How I Lost my Mom to Addiction—and Found the Road to Recovery

Jacq Maren

Some of my earliest memories are of my mom hanging out with her friends, drinking wine and getting tipsy.

When I was little, it didn't bother me—I just thought she and the other moms were having fun. Even better, we kids could pretty much get away with whatever we wanted as long as it didn't disrupt happy hour.

My parents divorced when I was eight and my dad passed away shortly after. This meant that my mom was a single parent to me and my two sisters, Grace and Jeanne. As the years progressed, my mom's drinking became more frequent; her behavior much more erratic and far less jovial. We found ourselves tiptoeing around the house, trying not to step on the landmines of her moods. When she was out of control, which was more often as the years went by, we learned to avoid her and fend for ourselves. I found myself endlessly trying to protect my sisters from the chaos, but I was just a kid.

Most of the time it felt like I was the parent to my mom and not the other way around.

It was exhausting. And lonely.

———

I had alcohol for the first time when I was 16. I was going on a flight alone—and I was terrified of flying.

"I can't do it," I told my mom, trembling as we got ready to leave for the airport. "I'm too scared."

"It's okay, honey," she said. "Drink this. It'll take the edge off." She produced a plastic cup with rose-colored wine in it, letting me sip in the back of the minivan all the way to the airport curb. It worked; I felt calm, warm and relaxed. From that day until I was in my 40s, I never got on a plane again without drinking.

My childhood was punctuated by a lot more than a fear of flying—I was constantly overwhelmed by nervousness, panic and anxiety (feelings later diagnosed as PTSD and depression). All I wanted to do was flee. In my teens, I threw myself into relationships of convenience, hoping the next guy would provide me an escape—another pattern that followed me well into adulthood.

My mom's behavior got even more unpredictable as I grew into a young woman. She became increasingly verbally and emotionally abusive, which I thought meant there was something deeply wrong with me. Over time, I got a nervous stomach whenever I saw my mom pouring herself a glass of wine. I didn't understand alcohol abuse the way I do now. I just knew that somehow the drinking made what was already bad so much worse.

I told myself I would never behave like my mom. No matter what happened, I would stay far, far away from alcohol. What was so great about it anyway?

———

At first, I kept my promise.

I didn't drink in high school.

Once I was in college, I learned to drink recreationally and enjoyed my fair share of pub crawls and spring break parties. The social drinking continued into my 20s, where I continued to have the girls' nights out, work happy hours and occasional glasses of wine with dinners—but all within healthy limits.

I wasn't living with my mom anymore, but her chaos still followed me. I spent the better part of my adult life paying off fraudulent charges she accrued under my identity. Well into my 30s, she would call at all hours of the night, threatening to harm herself or leaving unintelligible voice messages. Her episodes got so destructive that both my sisters and I went through various bouts of cutting her out of our lives for years at a time.

In 2004, I gave birth to my son, Jack. Two years later, I moved from Los Angeles to Kansas City to follow my then-husband's job and create a fresh start for our new family.

As much as I wanted this move to be a fairy tale, it quickly became a nightmare. Our marriage expired before the tags on my California plates. In no time, we were in the middle of an acrimonious divorce and I was a single parent raising a son in the middle of the country with no support system.

Alcohol became my stress reliever. I was no longer drinking to be social, I was doing it because I needed it: to relax, to calm my anxiety, to relieve the stress of everything that was my life.

There were times I questioned myself. I'd wonder if I was drinking too much, but then I'd look around at other moms and everyone else seemed to be doing it, too. Even at baby showers, kids' parties and soccer tournaments, moms were drinking wine by the bottle. I guess by then we'd all bought into the lie *Sex and the City* had sold on TV:

if you were a glamorous, independent woman who had her life together, you needed your glass as much as you needed your Gucci.

At first, I was just having a glass of wine at night to level out at the end of the day. Then one became three and three became four. Before too long, I was depending on it daily—to function, to numb, to sleep—all the while trying to keep it out of my son's sight.

It was exhausting. And lonely.

I was completely shocked to see myself repeating my mom's same destructive lifestyle, despite all efforts to the contrary. I embraced meditation, journaling and other healthy habits to turn things around—but I couldn't bring myself to embrace sobriety.

———

"I can't stop drinking," I blurted to my partner one day. I hadn't planned on saying it, but there it was.

I had already tried treatment for anxiety, depression and suicidal thoughts over the years, but none of it had been a long-term solution. Only when I went to intensive outpatient treatment did I start to heal from past trauma I'd never recognized or faced.

The ironic part was that around the same time, my mom was cutting back on drinking as well— though for more serious reasons. In 2016, after months in critical care from a near-fatal blood infection, she recovered—only to be diagnosed with colon cancer. She was cancer-free in 2017, but by 2019 it was back and more aggressive than before. She was in and out of the hospital constantly, and on so many medications that it had become impossible for her to drink—her doctors told her that doing so would be tantamount to suicide.

As an unexpected, yet welcome side effect, all of her unhealthy behaviors had seemingly disappeared overnight.

"I don't know what to tell you, Jacq," my sister Grace told me on a phone call one night. She was working and living in LA near my mom, so she was seeing things first-hand. "Mom is a different person. She's like the mom we always wanted."

I was hopeful but guarded. After all, I'd been through every emotion imaginable with my mom, from love and sympathy to hatred and resentment and back again. I was hesitant to open up to her again, but I had to. Just as my sister told me, Mom sounded calm, lucid and loving on the phone. Not just once, but every time I spoke to her. Grace was right. She was the mom I'd always wanted.

———

On the strength of our conversations, I flew out to LA to visit her in 2020.

I hadn't remained fully alcohol free in the years since I began my sobriety journey, despite going a year or more each time. I couldn't pinpoint why I would fall back into old habits—I just knew that the "pink cloud" eventually dissipated and I was left with myself again. And maybe that was the real problem to be faced.

Now that my mom was sober, albeit medically neces-sary, I thought that this may be my chance. I wanted to finally create some peace with her so I could forgive and heal. Maybe that was the missing piece.

When I arrived in California, my mom had just gone through another surgery and was bedridden. She'd also broken her wrist a day earlier in a bad fall. *This woman can't catch a break*, I thought.

One morning over coffee, I told her I wanted to talk to

her. I was so nervous I was nearly shaking, but I managed to open up about the pain of my childhood, how drinking had contributed and how I wanted to be transparent.

I braced myself for defensiveness, victimhood or an emotional explosion, but none of that happened. She just listened.

"You're right," she said quietly. "I was horrible to you."

Wait, I thought, *you already know that?* I wasn't prepared for her to speak so honestly about her own childhood, hidden pain and how she'd been drinking her whole life to self-medicate. I didn't even know that term was in her vocabulary.

She told me she'd had extremely low self-esteem since childhood and how failed relationships and single parenthood led to habitually abusing alcohol. Ouch. That sounded way too familiar.

"I never really did the things I wanted to do," she said sadly. "I was always sabotaging myself."

———

I'd always heard that alcoholism was cyclical, but I'd never understood what that meant. Because I grew up in chaos, I told myself I would never make the same mistakes—but I know now that's not true. In many cases, it's almost impossible not to.

My mom and I are very different people "on paper"— I'm very Type A. I color within the lines almost to a fault. She was an art student, living life as a true free spirit. Growing up, I thought she was crazy or deranged and that we were so different. I had no idea that beneath the drinking, we were so alike.

Witnessing my mother admit to the destruction of her addiction was nothing short of surreal. I always thought she would leave this earth without validating my pain and I'd be left with a gaping hole I didn't know how to fill. But I see the truth now: how addiction snuck up on my mother the same way it snuck up on me. Her transformation gave me perspective and hope. I knew I could keep pushing to live a sober life. She's proof that it's never too late.

I no longer want to punish my mother for the past; she's punished herself enough.

All that matters to us now is that we enjoy the time we have left together...and to share the story—our story—of the pain of addiction and the healing of recovery.

My Sober Sexual Awakening

Tawny Lara

I was a bonafide party girl for more than 10 years, personifying the stereotypes with slurred words and a boozy smile. I danced on bars, pursed my lips to make a duck face for pictures and loudly "whoooooooooed" anytime I ran into a friend I hadn't planned on seeing. My duck face may have looked like I was having the time of my life, but once my buzz wore off in the morning, it left me with a horrible headache. I was only slightly plugged into reality. It's hard to figure out who you are when you have a personality that's predominantly based on alcohol consumption. Alcohol amplified my people-pleasing tendencies—especially in the bedroom.

I've always had a dysfunctional relationship with sex that left me feeling simultaneously confident and insecure. Confident because I was down to try new positions with new partners. Insecure because much of that confidence came from a place of wanting to be perceived as cool, daring and sexy. That longing superseded my pursuit of genuine sexual satisfaction, bringing a performative element between the sheets. I knew I liked to explore and have fun, but I never took the time to get to know my own body until I got sober.

I had to get honest to admit that I had a drinking problem and that same level of honesty spread into every aspect of my life. Once I stopped lying to myself about my relationship with alcohol, it was hard to lie to myself about anything else. Removing booze from the equation pushed me to understand myself and the world in a new way. I couldn't hide from reality once sobriety fully plugged me into it. Sobriety is a fucking mirror, man.

One of the many lies I told myself and my sexual partners was about orgasms. I faked them. A lot. The gravity of this secret weighed heavily on me the first time I had sober sex. I was seeing someone for a month or so before we became sexual. The old me would have had sex, faked an orgasm and gone on with the rest our night. But this night was different since there was no alcohol involved. Inspired by the infamous *Seinfeld* scene when Elaine tells Jerry that she "fake fake fake faked" with him, I shared my secret with my date.

"I always fake orgasms when I have sex," I said.

"Why?" he asked, confused.

"I honestly don't know," I replied in earnest. "But I don't want to do it anymore."

"Sex is about more than orgasms," he assured me with a kiss. "It's about connection and fun. Let's just focus on that."

So that's just what we did: we focused on fun.

That was the first time I felt fully empowered in bed. I wasn't worried about how I looked. I didn't keep track of the time so I could begin my *performance*. I experienced the first sign of what I now recognize as intimacy. We had a good time and a genuine connection, no orgasms required.

The suffocating weight of carrying that lie finally began to dissipate. I was free.

I told him that I didn't know why I faked orgasms, but that wasn't true. I did know. I faked because I wanted to appear "normal"—whatever the hell that means. Film, television, and porn present the female orgasm in an incredibly unrealistic way. This conditioning convinced me that "normal" women climax often, and quickly, during sex—even without clitoral stimulation. It wasn't until later in sobriety, after obsessively researching the topic, that I discovered how common it actually is to fake orgasms.

As Lux Alptraum states in her book, *Faking It: The Lies Women Tell About Sex and the Truths They Reveal*, "Women lie because sometimes a lie is the only way to express a deeper truth."

Lying about my drinking problem and faking orgasms was how I expressed my deeper truth: I was terrified of getting to know the real me.

I also faked because I was more concerned with placating the male ego than pursuing my own pleasure. It just seemed easier to keep the lie going instead of facing why I lied in the first place. This lie also represented my sexuality, my womanhood and the faith I had in myself. The thought of confronting those parts of me seemed impossible. In fact, those were some of the topics I drank to hide from in the first place. Sobriety wouldn't let me hide anymore.

Hollywood doesn't only tell us how the female orgasm should look; it also shows us how a rock bottom should look. My rock bottom was not the dramatic I-lost-everything trope that you see on screen. In fact, it was pretty tame. Some co-workers and I met at Fanelli's in SoHo, our favorite spot. But something felt different this time. Perhaps on some level, I knew this was my last hoorah. The recurring theme in our conversation was the fact that we each moved to New York City to pursue our creative passions but we "didn't have enough time" to pursue those passions. I moved to New York City to find my voice as a writer, but I wasn't writing.

Four pints of Stella and Paulaner Hefeweizen later, we separated before walking to our respective trains. This is when I felt a shift. While I enjoyed my Sunday Funday beer buzz, I also became hyper-aware of the fact that we had just spent four hours in a pub...in Manhattan...drinking alcohol...talking about how we don't have enough time to accomplish the goals that brought us to Manhattan in the first place. Yet another example of how I lied to myself about my drinking problem. This reality check struck me; I couldn't shake it. In those four hours, the sunny afternoon transitioned into a haunting dusk while we transitioned from sober to beer buzzed. Bubbly to morose. This dusk, this buzz mocked me. It screamed —*Make a change*!

The next morning I woke up feeling groggy. Not quite hungover but not quite my usual, I-love-mornings self. I skipped my workout. Again. I stayed in bed to stare at the ceiling, waiting for something to jump out at me to explain why I felt so off. This familiar pseudo hangover felt like a strange mix of emotional and physical anguish.

To be honest, it never felt great after a night of drinking, but again, I was hyperaware this time. I walked to the bathroom to look at myself in the mirror: Bags under my eyes. Face bloated. Belly bloated. Mascara all around my eyes. Head cloudy. I thought, *You're 29. This isn't cute anymore.* At that moment I decided to not drink for a week.

I'd done this before. I'd even gone for three months without booze just to prove to myself I could do it, only to celebrate the three-month mark with shots of Jack Daniels.

One week turned into two weeks. Those two weeks turned into three weeks.

Then I made a decision that changed the entire trajectory of my life: *I'll be 30 next week. I'll celebrate by not drinking for the duration of my 30th year.* The gonzo journalist in me decided to take this plan a step further: *I'll document this entire experience, in real-time, by starting a blog.*

So I launched SobrieTeaParty.com. This solidified that pub conversation. If alcohol was getting in the way of my writing, I should stop drinking and write about it, right? My blog served as a form of accountability for both sobriety and writing. That year-long social experiment was the jumping-off point that I needed. As I write this, I have four-and-a-half years without a drink or drug.

After countless years of flirting with sobriety, I finally ditched booze for good. Perhaps it was that I had recently relocated from Texas to New York City. Or maybe it was the fact that I could no longer hide from how my drinking habits hindered my ability to take my writing—and myself—seriously. I think it was a bit of both. I had no idea that sobriety would make everything better: my writing, my mental health and my sexuality. Especially the latter.

In sobriety, I no longer wanted to add a performative element to sex. The thought of tightening my pelvic floor while gyrating my hips and moaning in pseudo-pleasure seemed like too much work. This lie I told myself and my sexual partners over 14 years of sexual activity finally felt dishonest. I've always enjoyed sex because it felt good. Why did I think that fake orgasms had to be part of the experience?

I replaced the bedroom performances with much-needed alone time to reintroduce myself to my body. I spent time discovering what I like, what I don't like and what I'd maybe like to try with someone else. I longed for genuine connection and intimacy with a partner who wanted to explore my body with me.

My plan was simple: give up booze and write about it for a year. That year changed the course of my life. Self-discovery and a sexual awakening came as a much-appreciated side effect of a sober life. I'm still a party girl, it's just that the party has changed. I actually remember what, and who, I did the night before.

No Is a Complete Sentence

Lauren Schwarzfeld

My drinking story isn't that dramatic. I didn't lose my car or my house or my children. I was never arrested. I never ended up in the ER. But I was uncomfortable in my own skin. I felt lost. I didn't know what I wanted. And I was sick of waking up with a shame-over, wondering what I'd done the night before.

There was no single catastrophic event that inspired me to stop drinking. There were years of deep thought about how my relationship with alcohol was unhealthy and then, finally, there was the last shameful morning when I woke up and thought, *I'm done.*

The alternative would have been to wait for a catastrophic event, but why? I realized that maybe I didn't need to lose everything in order to want more for myself. Maybe I didn't need to hit a low rock bottom. Maybe I could create my own bottom by making the decision to say one simple word.

No.

Before I started saying no, I was the person who said yes to everything.

I was a good kid, the kind of kid who did what she was supposed to. I grew up poor with a single mom. It forced me to be responsible. *Ish.* I understood how to make things look good.

In high school, I got a job at a restaurant. The food service world is not for 15-year-old girls, but there I was anyway, earning my own money for the very first time. I made friends with my coworkers, who were all older than me, and when we were finished with work, we'd go out drinking until the bars closed. We were the late crew.

"I'm spending the night at my friend's house, Mom!"

The restaurant job was my first big lesson in self-sufficiency. I learned that I could have whatever I wanted as long as I was willing to work for it. The way I understood life was like this: If I simply followed a series of logical steps, then I would get my desired outcome and be happy. And if I wasn't happy, then it was my fault.

In college, in addition to excessive drinking and experimenting with drugs, I continued to work hard. I had at least one part-time job at all times and, during the holidays, I'd work at the restaurant for extra cash. Money didn't just magically appear in my bank account like it did for my friends. Providing for myself was overwhelming sometimes, but I could handle it. I was in control of my life.

It was logical to major in finance and accounting because I was good at math and had tons of student loans to pay off. Did I enjoy the finance world? I never paused to ask myself this question. Every time I hated one of my jobs in finance, I was confused. Wasn't I supposed to be happy now?

Instead of asking myself what I wanted, I crowd-sourced all major life decisions.

"I don't know," I would say. "What do you think?"

I asked everyone this question.

I thought quitting the finance world was the answer. It wasn't. I thought being a stay-at-home mom would fix things. It didn't.

I spent years bouncing from one job to the next, saying yes to whatever came my way. I said yes to direct sales, real estate, becoming a doula and every volunteer opportunity that was presented. Even though each role spoke to me in some way, I hated them all because they just didn't fit. It never occurred to me to mold these opportunities to fit who I was. How could I? I had no idea who I was. I was too busy asking everyone else and accepting what was handed to me.

I was trying to find my voice, but my voice was drowned out by everybody else's voices.

I learned that the more desperate I became for guidance, the less discerning I was about where it came from. I made the mistake of listening to one very powerful voice.

When I felt weakest, I looked for strength. And that strength took the form of a new best friend, who also happened to be a narcissist.

I was lost, she was strong.

I was miserable, she had the answers.

I was failing, she kept score.

I felt a constant reminder of everything I wasn't. Of all the things I should or could be—if only I worked harder for them. *Maybe I just don't like being a mom*, I thought. *Maybe I just don't like being married.*

I felt guilty and then I felt selfish for feeling guilty. In a nutshell, I felt like shit, and when you feel like shit, why not drink excessively?

———

I was a sloppy drunk. It was routine for me to wake up in the morning and check my sent messages and my socials with a sense of dread. Had I said anything stupid? Posted anything inappropriate? Who had I run into?

It started to feel exhausting, but I didn't know how to change. Drinking was part of my identity and yet, I was beginning to hate everything about it.

Before I could cut out alcohol completely, I tried to control it. I made rules. *No martinis until dark. A glass of rosé during the day has to have ice in it.* Every time I made a new rule, I quickly came up with excuses to break it. Because in the summer, it didn't get dark until nine. Was I really going to wait until nine to have a martini? There was a period of time when I casually did cocaine (a college favorite)—but only on vacation. Still, if the kids went to my mom's house, then wasn't that like a vacation?

Making and breaking my own rules was useless, because the problem was not the alcohol. It was me. I couldn't drink like a normal person.

———

When my toxic relationship with the narcissistic friend ended, I felt a heavy weight lifted off my shoulders. I was freeing myself from the pressure of other people's expectations. I was quieting the noise I shouldn't have listened to. I was dropping the weight of answers that weren't intended for me. In the aftermath, I had to seriously ask myself why I'd sought out and strived to follow guidance when it always made me feel so terrible.

It finally hit home that I needed to stop asking other people what I should be doing with my life and start asking myself. I'd been comparing myself to other people, feeling guilty that I wasn't them. But why would I want to be anybody other than myself?

Before I said no to drinking, I started saying no to other things. No, I realized, I didn't want to be the same kind of mother as my friend, and so I didn't have to be. She loved cooking and I did not and therefore no, I would not cook unless I had to. I could get takeout instead. And my sister could craft with the kids because she loved crafting and I didn't. Unapologetically, I started outsourcing the things I didn't want to do. These early practices at saying no were what eventually gave me the confidence to say no to alcohol.

I spent a year and a half intensely wondering what it would be like not to drink before I stopped. I played out scenarios in my head. What would it be like to go on a vacation? What would it be like to go out to dinner with my friends? How would my life look if I were participating without a drink in my hand?

November 11, 2017 was a non-eventful day. We had a bunch of people over and I drank some champagne. At the time, that meant two bottles. I felt funny and charming. I woke up the following morning and for whatever reason, this was when I got it. I thought, *I am not funny and charming. I'm annoying and a drunk. I am done.*

Later that week, I went out to dinner with three friends. They all ordered drinks. I lied to get out of it. "I've had a headache all day," I said, "I'm not going to drink."

After that, I was like, *Okay, I just had dinner and didn't drink and it wasn't weird.*

The days kept adding up. I told a friend, "I haven't had a drink in a week and a half and I think I'm going to stop."

My friend didn't care at all about my huge life-changing decision. "That's cool," she said.

That Thanksgiving was the first I'd spent sober since I was probably 12 years old. Afterwards, I thought, *Okay, I can successfully not drink during a holiday.*

Then Christmas came. Another holiday sober.

It wasn't until January that I started saying, "I don't drink." Before then I'd made it sound kind of temporary. "I'm not drinking tonight." I realized that I didn't need to make up excuses about headaches. I didn't need to apologize or explain.

After so many years of wandering around my life shamelessly unsure of what to do next, I was defining what I wanted by defining what I didn't want. Saying no to drinking was huge. After that, I realized I could say no to anything.

I'd been drowning in volunteer duties, so I simply started to decline them.

"Do you make an excuse?" my husband asked me one night.

"I just say no."

No is a complete sentence.

Last Thanksgiving, I woke up in the morning shame-free and drove to pick up a turkey that had been cooked by somebody else. We had 27 people at our house and not a single dish had been cooked in our oven. That made me so happy.

"Must be nice," people have said to me many times. My response to that is yes, it is very nice. I grew up poor and I know exactly how nice it is. I'm not sorry.

Another thing people often say to me is how they wish

they could drink less. "I drank a bottle of wine last night. I wish I could do what you do."

Feeling confident enough to do what I want regardless of what other people are doing has given me so much freedom. When I'm listening to my own voice, things seem to unfold in my favor.

I've wanted to be a writer since I was a kid. For the longest time, I thought about starting a blog. But who would proofread it for me? Who would tell me whatever I'd written was okay? And also, what was the point of a blog? If there was no logical reason to do it, then why do it?

I realized that there didn't need to be a logical reason. I could do it just because I wanted.

In addition to my own blog, I also write for a mom blog in Westchester County. My post about not drinking got by far the most views of any post I've ever written. This makes me realize that people are curious about the alcohol-free life. I imagine many of my readers are women who live in Westchester like me. Maybe they're moms who drink rosé, which is who I used to be. And maybe if I keep putting myself out there, I can help one of these women if she wants to stop.

I used to think, *I know people in the world don't drink, but where are they?*

Not drinking is still out of the norm. Most people drink. And it's very easy to get caught up in what society expects from us. It's very easy to keep doing what we think we're supposed to.

It's also, as it turns out, easy to say no.

Everything is Awful... Or Is it?

Sean Paul Mahoney

Worst year ever. Worst day ever. Worst Oscars ever. Worst Super Bowl ever. Worst election ever. Worst whatever ever. It seems like everything I turn on or log on to or listen to is telling me how hard life is right now. Oh, and it's been like this for a while. The overwhelming message being blasted out of life's speakers 24 hours a day is that life is terrible and every day is a struggle. In fact, our common distaste for how allegedly crappy everything is binds us all together but not in a good way.

Recently, I spent time with some coworkers bitching about everything. And I mean everything—politics, our fellow co-workers, our workplace, you name it. I left feeling like I needed to douse my ears with bleach and watch 40 continuous hours of classic Hollywood musicals just to get the sour negativity taste out of my mouth. Granted, it has been a challenging time. There's a lot to worry about and grieve. Personally, my own life has been put through the juicer more than once and my head has been left spinning and heavy. Yet there's something inherently contradictory about being in recovery and buying into this "The whole world is terrible!" narrative.

I know just as well as everyone else that it's hard to stay positive about the state of the human race. I am, after all, a homosexual male of Irish descent in his 40s who is also a writer, so being bitter and jaded about the world is one of my default settings. But even I'm not buying this massive craptastic blanket we've put on the state of the world.

First of all, I feel like anybody who's lived through the horrors of addiction and alcoholism knows what real hell looks like. Sure, right now might not be the most fun time period in human history but compared to waking up hungover and wanting to die like I did seven days a week for over 10 years, it's a walk in the park. Honestly. Give me the choice of daily drinking again and living through this past year and I'll gladly choose the latter. What I'm saying is a little perspective is needed when we go down this abyss of despair. I kicked a daily cocaine habit, quit drinking and left a toxic relationship, for goodness sakes. The world being in the crapper is something I can handle. In fact, if anybody should be called on in our troubled times, I think it should be people in recovery. We've already seen it all and gotten out on the other side. We got this. Our strength, humor and "girl, calm down" demeanor could really be of service to normies.

Speaking of perspective, it helps me to remember that any day I stay sober is a pretty great day. I know. I know. Feel free to throw your laptop at that statement. Lord knows I nearly hung up on my sober bestie when he said, trying to comfort me in my first year, "Sometimes all we get is to stay sober." But it's true. Staying sober is huge especially when the world stinks and people are the worst. Yet here we are and this is the only option, I mean the only real option that won't kill me.

When I first started going to meetings in Santa Monica, like clockwork somebody would always say, "We don't pick up, no matter what." I heard that over and over again and I'm thankful I did, even if I rolled my eyes at the time. Because what this whole not picking up no matter what gig means is that I can't drink over the state of the world, over humanity going to hell, over the president, over anything. I get to be sober and present for all of it—yippee. I joke but it is an enormous gift. I've recently watched as people still active in their addictions try to process the wacky world around them and it is not pretty. They keep pouring booze and drugs on their lives in hopes that it'll make the world go away but it never works. Never worked for me either.

Also? I would make a strong argument for the world not really being that awful to begin with. Here are a few positives: pandas are no longer endangered, the Earth actually has a second moon and new HIV treatments are pushing the world closer to a cure. Fantastic, but we can go deeper. If you aren't one of the 52,000 people who died of an opiate overdose in the last year then you are doing alright. Likewise, if you weren't one of the 88,000 people to die in an alcohol-related death, you are rocking it. But I really think we can do even better. If you stayed sober, if you helped other addicts, if you didn't drink or use even though things were rough, I love your life. Hell, I want your life. By staying sober your existence is already better than it was and exponentially more awesome than most.

Okay, so what if we buy this revolutionary idea that life is actually okay? How do we deal with the ever-engulfing black hole of negativity closing in around us? I'm really not sure. Sorry. I'm not. For what it's worth, I think a little cynicism in small doses is okay. I'm a card-carrying smartass who personally gets a lot comfort out of being able to laugh at the world and the people in it.

I also know things are less hideous when I'm not a total jerk. Little stuff like taking care of myself, getting enough sleep and eating something delicious can help. Those steps ensure that I won't act like a total nightmare and ruin everyone's day around me. When none of that works and my attitude still sucks, I have to pull out the big guns. No, not literally. I mean I have do something really hard: think of someone other than myself. I know. Drag. But it works every time. Texting another addict, showing up to a meeting or just laughing with a group of sober people makes the world a little less awful.

Now, just imagine how un-awful everything would be if we all did that at the same time.

An Act of Love

Colleen Connaughton

Asking the NYPD to lock my brother up was an agonizing decision. But after months of research and debate, I finally did it.

Hi, my name is Colleen Connaughton. My brother is an NYPD officer in Queens. I was referred to you by a professional interventionist who said you could stage an intervention. He has a serious gambling addiction. I fear for his life and his family's safety and I am hoping he can get the help he needs now. I've been assured that the NYPD are pros at this. I know you have the programs and leverage to make recovery work. I love him dearly. Our deceased mother's dying wish was to get him into treatment. So can you help him?

The day I made this request was one of the saddest of my life. I had the sense that my heart was falling to the floor. I could barely breathe.

Michael may never view my attempt to help him as the act of love that it truly was, but I had no other choice.

———

"Please don't let your brother fall. When the time comes, rescue him."

This is what my mother said to me as she lay dying of cancer.

Someday, she said, Michael would need my help. He would need me to be strong for him. "Will you help him?" she asked.

My mother was an alcoholic. Ironically, Michael and I had staged an intervention for her a few years earlier. It was successful. She stopped drinking.

Michael's problem wasn't drinking. It was gambling. Over the years, he'd gotten himself into increasingly impossible situations and then asked our mother to bail him out.

"I'll help him," I promised. And mentally, I prepared for the next crisis. When the bookies came calling again, I would come to his rescue. "But I'm not going to cover it up for him," I said.

I refused to continue our family's legacy of shame and secrecy around addiction. "I'm going to help him through tough love and full exposure." I wanted to break the cycle of addiction in our family so it would not pass on to my sons or Michael's daughters. I felt it was important to show them that addiction is nothing to be ashamed of; it's an illness that is curable.

I sat on the edge of my mother's hospital bed holding her hand. Her eyes were bloodshot from pain medication and from the exhausting process of a long, slow death. She teared up at my response. She was crying because she knew how painful it would be for my brother to be exposed. The consequences would be brutal.

Michael was the father of two beautiful girls and a NYPD officer. If mishandled, the intervention could cause him to lose his job and pension.

I could see all these fears in my mother's eyes and feel them in her body language.

She looked at her hands and said, "I'm sorry I let you down with my drinking and now I leave this for you to handle."

At that, I broke down and sobbed uncontrollably. They were all the tears I'd pent up during the months of watching her suffer as disease ravaged her body and spirit. But mostly I wept over the fact that I'd made my fun-loving, quirky lovable mom cry by telling her I was going to be tough on my brother, her beloved son. Maybe I should have sugar-coated the truth, but I was angry—angry about how addiction had tainted our otherwise loving family and angry that I would have to hurt Michael in order to help him when the time came.

I hugged my mom and told her not to apologize. She'd been a heroic single mother, working nights as a dispatcher at LaGuardia and never complaining. I told her she had been the best mother we could hope for and had given us unconditional love and freedom. I thanked her for all of it.

My mother comforted me as only a mother could. Her arms around me felt so safe and secure. I assured her again that I would take care of Michael.

Two weeks later, she passed away.

————

Several years after my mother died, Michael hit a low point. He was waking up in the middle of the night, sweating profusely, anxious about his increasing debts and the bookies who were after him. He couldn't stop going to the track and he'd started drinking more. He begged me for $10,000. I just didn't have it. His friends didn't have it either—he'd called them, too.

First, I went to his wife and asked her to help. Would she join me in staging an intervention? She told me to stay out of it. She didn't want to compromise his pension plan. "You're not his mother," she reminded me. "Your brother is an addict. He will always be an addict. I have to worry about my daughters."

"I know," I said, "but I don't want him to die."

This is when I began the process of staging the intervention. I planned it meticulously so that Michael wouldn't lose his job or pension. I wanted him to get better. I didn't want him to suffer. I checked with former NYPD officers who had been put into rehab by NYPD, I consulted the head of Gamblers Anonymous NY, I paid to get advice from the nation's leading expert on gambling addiction. I did every single thing possible to make sure I was right and it would work.

During the planning, I sought comfort and advice from longtime friends. They'd been our neighbors growing up. We were so close that we considered them to be part of our family. The daughter had been my maid of honor—she was like a sister and her brother was like my brother. We spent Thanksgivings, Christmas parties, christenings and weddings together. Their mother was my mother's close friend; she'd helped my mother during her chemo.

Over the years, this family had helped Michael many times in exchange for favors—they bailed Michael out of his gambling debts (with the bookies) and got him jobs. Michael, in return, fixed tickets for our old neighbors and their friends. It was a mutually beneficial relationship.

For months, the family listened to my plans about the intervention and said they wanted to help. It was a relief to know that.

It was even more of a relief when, the night before the intervention, the NYPD told me, "Don't worry, we've got everything set up." A weight was lifted off my shoulders. The next day, I would be free.

———

But on the day of the intervention, the family friends sent an attorney to stop it. Their mutually beneficial relationship would no longer be useful if Michael were in treatment. And they probably worried that Michael would tell all the secrets about their illicit dealings.

Instead of an intervention, this family helped Michael get out of debt, retire early from the NYPD and get a new job.

I, meanwhile, was discredited, vilified and completely cut off. I haven't heard from anyone in their family. Michael, who lives five blocks away, refuses to speak to me. When I see him around town, he ignores me. I don't see his daughters anymore, or his wife. My mother would be heartbroken to know we are estranged.

———

Mine is an extreme example of how trying to get an addict help can backfire. In Al-Anon, they tell you to stay in your own lane and focus on yourself. But how do you sit back and watch someone you love slowly die? It's very difficult not to intervene.

I felt obligated to try to help, although the trying drained me. Michael's addiction drained me, too, just like my mother's had. I was worried about him all the time. When the intervention was blocked, I felt betrayed and amazingly disappointed. In the aftermath and still now, it's sad to think of all the relationships I've lost.

Secrets keep us sick. Growing up in an Irish Catholic alcoholic household, I learned early on that appearances were more important than the truth. Don't talk about the problem. Don't expose the family. Those were the lessons I was taught. I wanted to break our family's cycle of addiction in this generation.

Michael's intervention was my attempt to do it differently. I hoped it would give my brother—a humble, great guy—a path toward recovery. But life has not worked out that way.

Soon after the failed intervention, I contacted our old family friends and said, "You better make sure that all his debts are paid and his children are safe. You are responsible now."

It's a bittersweet relief to feel like I am no longer in charge of what happens to my brother. We always got along well, had both helped our mother die and shared that grief. He is the person who knows me longest in this world—and that is lost.

———

My mother truly was the best mother we could have hoped for. She was only 20 when she had us and worked hard at parenting. I have wonderful memories of Michael, my mother and myself, parading around New York as a gleeful little trio. Too poor to afford a car, we rode bicycles through the streets of Queens and took the subway to Central Park for picnics. She used to save milk carton coupons to get us free Mets baseball tickets. She threw the best ice cream sundae parties.

Yes, she also drank. It made my childhood difficult and confusing in certain ways. She started drinking when we were about 10, so it was our high school years that were affected; then she got sober.

And then she passed away.

I would be lying if I said that I don't feel like I've failed her.

But at least I know I tried.

How I Learned to Break the Cycle of Silence and Violence—in Jail

Christy Leis

It's usually men who are arrested for domestic violence, but I was the exception to the rule.

It was 2012 and I was living in Sunnyvale, California. Life was as stressful as it had ever been. I had just moved from LA, where I lived for eight years, with a big hole in my work history. Though I got a master's degree in speech pathology in 1997, I stopped working to stay home and raise my children.

I was in a new city, struggling to be a good parent, make money and balance my marriage simultaneously. My husband and I were fighting more frequently and the fights were getting increasingly intense. During one in particular, things got physical, and my husband called the cops.

When the police pulled up, I hadn't had time to comb my hair and I looked like a mad woman. Though we'd both contributed to the fight, the police decided to take only me to jail.

"You're arresting me? Are you kidding me?" I said mostly to myself, shaking my bowed head in disbelief.

"I don't belong in jail—I work with kids with disabilities!" Though that was true, they didn't seem to hear me and it didn't matter.

As a brown girl raised in a family that worked in public safety, I knew to hide any anger I felt or objections I had—they would only make things harder on me. I was stunned into inaction and disbelief, but they continued to cuff me in my living room, reciting my rights. After that, they loaded me in the back of their unmarked white van and I crumpled in the backseat.

Jail was immediately unlike anything I'd ever experienced. I couldn't even step over a painted line without being yelled at and threatened by guards. It was scary, but I quickly saw that for some of the women in there, this was their entire life. It became clear when I overheard a woman talking about her daughter.

"She's getting so big," she said with a sad smile. She had a picture above her bunk she was pointing to, showing another inmate. "I'm glad she's being raised by her father and his new girlfriend." It was heart-rending but inside, I shuddered. I couldn't imagine myself ever being glad that someone else was raising my child.

The next surprise came while I was in line for food. I had no appetite and one of the women came up to ask if she could eat my portion. I said yes and she looked me up and down. "Haven't I seen you before?" She asked me. I froze—didn't she know that I didn't belong here? That I had been a good person my whole life?

"I've been around," I said offhandedly, putting on a front. The entire exchange was surreal—I was angry and frustrated and wanted out, but what I hadn't expected was the calmness that came over me. I couldn't believe where I'd ended up, but on some level, I was shocked at how comfortable I felt. How easily I fit in.

I'd spent my whole life trying to fit in the white professional world outside and still always felt different. In Santa Clara County jail that day, that old label of "upstanding citizen" was rendered null and void in an instant. Amidst so many other brown bodies, I blended right in and "belonged." If just a few things in my life had gone differently, jail could've been my entire world, too.

———

Growing up, my parents hadn't been violent with each other. My mom was quiet and controlling, and she and my dad would fight—it would just happen behind closed doors. The unintended result was that my siblings and I never saw them negotiating or peacefully resolving things with one another.

As my siblings and I grew into our own adult relationships, we inherited their behavior. For some of us, it meant punching holes in walls and doors during domestic disputes. For me, it meant I had license to fight back—physically.

Because many of the men in my life had been angry and volatile, the women sometimes hit them in retaliation and felt safe doing so because they were smaller. In my own marriage, I'm only 5'2" and my husband was more than six feet tall. Using my inherited logic, whatever I did to fight him seemed totally defensible. As crazy as it sounds, in my family, it was normalized. I didn't know until later that this thinking went even further back than my parents.

My dad's earliest memory was waking up at four years old to his dad pointing a gun at his mom. When he told me, I was shocked. As I knew him, my grandfather was a tiny Filipino man who often worked in his garden throughout my childhood. How could a person so gentle get so angry at someone? My family always said my grand-mother was "crazy." As an adult, I understood differently. She was another woman of color who wanted to break free.

———

My grandfather came to America directly from the Philip-pines in the 1920s. When I was growing up, he told me a lot of stories about being treated badly by white people. Although my Filipino family had been college-educated, when they got here, their education and prestige had been instantly invalidated. At home, he was primed to be a lawyer; in America, he had to take what he could get.

In his first week, he was in a breadline and competing for jobs well below his station.

Over time, I saw my entire family was incredibly gifted. My extended relatives were all talented teachers. My sister is beyond artistic, and my mom could make anything with her hands. Even my grandfather had an angelic voice, though I've only ever heard him sing once, in a church. When they came here, all those voices were silenced. Racism offered up its own labels, labels my family came to believe and accept.

To this day, I'm still one of just three in my generation to graduate from college in America—I'm also the only one with a master's degree. As I thought about it in jail, I understood my grandfather's rage. When people treat you a certain way and there's no recourse, that anger has to go somewhere.

In my first marriage, I had started unconsciously repeating codependent patterns my parents had shown me. My husband was a boisterous white man and I was just a small brown girl. It was impossible not to notice how his stature and skin color opened doors for me—it was a view into a world of relative ease and advantage.

Initially, I liked that my husband was loud and confident where I was meek and quiet. Over time, it started to tear us apart. He got more successful at his job, and before long, I was alone with the kids, full of sadness and resentment. I was dependent on him and didn't have to work, but the exchange had been to make myself small, to put my ambitions on hold. After 11 years, we divorced.

I couldn't communicate my wants and needs or stand up for myself. I thought I'd learned, but here I was in another shaky relationship, repeating the same patterns. Where does this all end? I wondered. Had codependency really led me here?

———

Even in the white-dominated field of speech pathology, I never quite felt like I fit in. My upbringing had left me feeling like my opportunities were limited, like I had to lean on institutions and other powerful people to speak for me or allow me access. I had done the "right" things, but my positive labels hadn't saved me. I was still in jail with other women who were mothers and daughters just like me.

When the time came, I finally got my phone call. The phone was dirty and the call had to be made collect, so I called my parents and hoped they would answer. I'd told my mom earlier that day that my husband and I had been fighting, so right away, she was yelling at me.

"I don't need this right now," I said. "I need you to get me out of here!" I told her about the fight and how I had just been defending myself, but as I told it, I realized it didn't ring true anymore. I was telling it as a victim. I had only been in jail for five hours when my mom bailed me out.

Even in that limited time, my perspective had changed forever.

———

As a woman of color, I know there are larger forces working against me beyond my control. My grandparents took risks coming to America for opportunities, but they were unprepared for what they would face. In some ways, that promise of opportunity turned into intergenerational trauma—trauma I was now staring down and reliving. I knew I had to take ownership of turning that trend around for myself, and to help others, by example, to do the same.

Today, I consistently attend twice weekly CoDA meetings. I'm unlearning the allure of unhealthy relationships and codependency. I'm focused on asking for what I need, using my gifts to their fullest potential and living authentically no matter what I face. Though I may feel shame for my mistakes, I'm also grateful for the perspective I've gained.

Above all, I'm learning that I must still claim agency in my own life. By working my program and being mindful, by practicing compassionate inquiry and choosing my own labels, I know can heal—and this way, I can still fight back.

The Farm That Made Me into a Man

Paul Roux

I had my first real drink when I was 15.

I was in a boarding school near an affluent suburb in Pretoria, South Africa when my friends and I jumped the fence on Wednesday night and snuck to a bar around the corner for shots of tequila. After just a few shots, I felt the warm buzz and was relaxed and happy—it was a feeling of freedom I didn't know I'd been looking for.

Until that point, I felt somehow disconnected from everybody else. It seemed everyone in my life was "in" on something I was excluded from, but alcohol had changed that. It was a new feeling, and I wanted more of it.

The first time I got drunk, I was 17 at a school dance and I blacked out. My friends told me I'd been out of control, hanging off people and saying embarrassing things. I felt shame and embarrassment the next day, but I shrugged it off. It was normal to drink too much once in a while, I figured.

Getting a formal diagnosis of depression at 18 was a confirmation I was different, and it gave me another excuse to drink. *Of course, I have to drink all the time*, I thought to myself. *I have depression.*

With that, I started taking anti-depressants, but I didn't stop drinking.

———

In college, I would get drunk and insist on driving, wrestling my keys away from well-meaning friends. Getting pulled over by police officers for driving drunk didn't stop me—I somehow managed to bribe my way out of trouble for it whenever I got caught. No matter how many car accidents I got into (and there were several), I thought it was all just part of being a wild kid.

When I graduated the pattern continued. I got a full-time job at a bank and on weekends, would drink more with diminishing returns.

I was in pain nearly all the time and I started to realize I might need a change of environment and some new friends. Maybe then my life would be better.

I moved to Canada to be near some extended family, but the change had no remedial effects. If anything, my behavior was getting more dangerous. Soon I was smoking weed to take the edge off my hangovers, which were getting worse. On big nights out, I'd do whatever other drugs were around, including cocaine. The tipping point came when I blacked out on a subway train in Toronto and woke up on the platform alone, asleep on a bench. My phone, wallet and jacket were gone. I'd been robbed.

———

After three years at my job in Canada, I quit and moved back to South Africa to be with my family. I was scared of myself, but I wasn't ready to stop—and moving back in with my parents wasn't the break I thought it would be.

"What is that smell?" My mom would ask me, sniffing the air theatrically. "It smells like weed, Paul. Do you smell that?" Inside I boiled with paranoia and anger. All I could do was say I didn't smell anything and stomp out of the living room.

Of course, I smelled it—I was ducking out of the house or taking drives to get high all the time, sneaking around and hoping not to be called out. My parents would never say anything to me directly, but things in the house were getting more tense by the day. My mom's patience was wearing thin and my dad was spending more and more time in his office.

One day, my parents sat me down at the kitchen table and laid out my options.

"You need to sort yourself out," my dad said. "Your mom and I have been thinking about a solution to some of your problems."

What came next was ridiculous in hindsight. The first option was that I could go join a monastery in Italy to iron myself out. The second was that I could go to China to study martial arts at a camp. The third was that I could go to Resurrection Ministries, a working farm and a Christian rehab.

I wasn't sure about any of it, but I was out of chances. Rehab seemed like the best choice.

————

Getting to the farm put my privileged life in perspective immediately.

From the very first day, I was put on pig duty, ordered to root around in the mud with hordes of snorting hogs, shoveling shit. And these were enormous pigs.

One of the other guests told me before I'd arrived, one of the pigs had flipped a 100-pound bag of concrete mix into the air with its snout. It fell on another pig, killing it instantly.

I was in a world unlike any I'd been in before. Every day, we were expected to be up at 4:45 am without alarm clocks. If any of us were late, nobody got morning tea. It was the only comfort we were allowed, so getting it was a big deal...unfortunately, I was late a lot and the group started to turn on me. In the fields, there were snakes everywhere. There were electric fences to keep out animals. There were cows with massive horns, ready to charge and gore you. My life flashed before my eyes multiple times a week there.

Every day, the people in charge and the other guests called me out on my bad attitude. I was lacking an "attitude of gratitude" for our cigarette rationing system and made the mistake of showing the owner as much—and she chewed me out so loudly that everyone in the valley could hear it. The other guests complained about my bad cooking—hell, before rehab, I could barely chop an onion. Wherever I turned, I was getting broken down. There was no salvation coming, and everything was new, uncomfortable and awkward. I hated it.

———

After the first six weeks, I was finally allowed to have contact with my family again, and my parents scheduled a visit about a month or so later. The prospect was both exciting and terrifying. To compound my anxiety, I was wrestling with step three: turning my will and life over to God, which I stubbornly refused to do. All I wanted was to get out of there and go back to my old life.

One day, the owners approached me with an unusual request. "Can we pray for you?" I was taken aback. I wasn't getting on with the people who ran the ministry, but I wasn't particularly getting on with anyone else either. Even so, here they were, inviting me in. The prayer aspect seemed strange, but I didn't have a lot of people in my life showing me much love up to that point, so I said yes. With that, the group gathered around me with bowed heads and outstretched arms.

They prayed for God's peace to come down and for the Holy Spirit to move through me. *Fat chance*, I thought. Like always, my mental chatter was incessant and the volume knob was cranked to 11.

But something remarkable happened. I felt something. Something was flowing through me, calm and transcendent. For the first time I could remember, the chatter was quiet.

That night, I even shocked myself while journaling. *Today was the happiest day of my life*, I wrote. Before that day, I'd have called you a liar if you'd said the same thing to me.

———

When I was finally face-to-face with my parents, I could tell what a toll my behavior had taken on them. I was mostly glad to see them.

"I can't wait to get home again," I said. Their faces went blank.

"You're not coming home," my dad said. "You're not

staying with us anymore. You need to get a job and be a productive member of society." My final safe place had been removed.

After my parents left, there was more work to do. I thought I'd be out of the program in just a few months, but I wasn't ready. Soon the program's recommended six months were behind me as well. All I knew was I had to keep going. I had a lot of things to unlearn.

After 10 or 12 months, I broke down and told my parents everything—all the drugs I'd done, all the mistakes I'd made and how often. For the first time, I was letting them in. Maybe I'd been wrong about the world leaving me out of things my whole life. Maybe the problem was that I couldn't be honest and open with myself, so I couldn't be honest and open with others.

I'd been hiding from life, but I decided to stay as long as it took to learn not to hide anymore. Even in the darkest valleys, I felt some benevolent force urging me on. It ended up taking 18 months.

———

As it turned out, rehab life was not so different from sober, mature adult life on the outside.

When I left rehab, I got two jobs waiting tables, covering all seven days of the week. I was relieved to see my parents were still there to help me, despite everything. They lent me an old car and I had just enough cash flow to fill it, eat, pay rent and repeat. I got up at dawn, worked nonstop and ate plenty of instant noodles and beans.

I was working my program in earnest, going to meetings, talking to my sponsor and above all praying to God. At work, I served customers, washed dishes and scrubbed floors. It wasn't glamorous, but I was at peace. I could finally see my life unfurling in front of me.

Despite having very little, I had been blessed with a renewed purpose. I was grateful for what I did have. For the first time, I was actually a part of my life, and God was at the center.

Chain Gang Swimsuit

Becky J. Sasso

I quit drinking and drugs on September 13, 2001. Everything in the world changed that week. It was a total fucking mess.

I lived in Olympia, Washington during the worst of my addiction. I use the term "live" loosely—mostly I was failing at life. I dropped out of college to be a full-time bartender and party girl. I was stealing money from my employer to support my drug habit and was perpetually about five minutes from getting fired, arrested and evicted from my apartment. My boyfriend had just checked into rehab—again. My ancient Volvo was held together with duct tape and guitar strings. That was just the surface stuff. I started to realize I was running out of options and decided to move home.

On the outside, my childhood probably looked fine. I had great clothes and went to nice schools. I got good grades without really trying and was decent at sports. It's a funny misconception that middle class kids, especially those from two-parent families, by default have stable childhoods. Our home actually had a lot of hidden dysfunction.

My parents spent most of their time apart—or fighting. They were also both very driven, more focused on their own goals and projects than the family. They were gone a lot. My older brother was really sick—physically and mentally—and that consumed everybody. I felt very isolated.

I always say my first drug was fantasy. I loved to read and would get totally lost in stories. I hated my reality. I was bored and lonely most of the time, so I loved to pretend and tell lies. The first time I was really drunk was the summer I was 13. It was another escape—I did my very best to make it a regular thing after that.

I got caught drinking at school when I was 14. This was in the days before metal detectors and electronic attendance records. I would leave campus at lunch and come back drunk—if I came back at all.

It occurred to me then that other kids didn't drink the way I did—like during school hours—but I didn't see it as a problem. I just got better at hiding it and sought older friends who liked to party.

I never drank like a normal person; I was extreme. When other kids were chugging beers, I was chugging vodka. When the people at the party were smoking pot, I was tripping on acid and sneaking off to snort coke. When I started hanging with people who thought it was okay to snort coke, I was the one shooting up heroin in the bathroom.

At first, I told myself that I was just young, wild and free. It was the Pacific Northwest in the 90s, heroin was just the whole vibe—the zeitgeist. There was a great music scene (the people who weren't there called it "grunge") and the drinking and drugs were a big part of that. It was easy to rationalize and glamorize the behavior—even the hard drugs—when so many people were doing it.

After a while that excuse stopped working (even on myself) and it was just obvious I had a problem. By then, my friends were going to jail, they were dying from the drugs and the lifestyle. I was so wrapped up in the disease that it wasn't about the college, art or the music scene anymore. I just stayed stuck in a spiral of self-loathing. I hated how I was living, so I used more to numb out, so I hated myself more, so I used more and so on.

The summer I was 24, I was a bridesmaid in my friend's wedding. I was dope sick, so I left the reception early to score drugs in a convenience store parking lot. I was high and probably a little drunk, wearing a long formal gown, with bruises and bloody sores on my arms, eating chocolate donuts. It was the first food I had all day. In that moment, some part of me looked at myself as an outsider and felt so sorry for that girl.

It was my moment of clarity.

I was past the point of making myself cute, pretending to be a regular person. I was just an emaciated, bruised, strung out girl, with questionable facial piercings, who hadn't had a haircut in a year. I was sick of the daily ritual of painting makeup on my wrists, hands and arms to cover my tracks.

I kicked heroin for the last time in my childhood bedroom Labor Day weekend, 2001. Meds kept me groggy, but did nothing to stop the shakes, sweats, blinding jolts of pain and days of hallucinations of spiders crawling all over my body. I basically spent about 10 days shitting, sleeping and crying.

Once I finished detox, I started a year-long Intensive Outpatient Program (IOP). I also went to an NA meeting every single day for my first three years of recovery. After I settled in, meetings were the place I felt safest in the beginning.

When I was nine months clean, I got arrested in my red swimsuit on my way to a recovery picnic. I was riding without a seatbelt in the back of a Jeep and they took me to jail because of some old warrants in another county. I figured I could handle the pesky warrants when I got to Step Eight, but that's not how it worked out.

I spent about a week in jail and rode with the chain gang across the state of Washington. For those who don't know, a chain gang is a bus full of criminals, cuffed and chained together, being transported to join a work crew or face charges in other jurisdictions.

After a weekend in a holding cell with eight other women, I was still in my red swimsuit and a teeny jean skirt —no actual shirt. Side note: Have you ever had to pee in a one-piece swimsuit? In a room full of people? The cops claimed I couldn't have a jail jumpsuit until I was officially booked in the county where I was being charged. That was probably bullshit...they were just enjoying my Pam Anderson *Baywatch*-style one piece along with a bus full of creepy murderer rapists.

That experience happened at a time when I was feeling a bit ambivalent about my new recovery. I was on the fence, thinking maybe I had a little game left—maybe it would be different this time and I could just drink a little— like a normal grown-up lady. Then I got arrested and my nine months of going to meetings every day and working the steps kicked in. I surrendered. My life was improving, present situation excluded. I practiced praying, I talked to the other women in jail about recovery. I tried hard during those days to find the positive and the lesson in the midst of the mess.

The most valuable realization came to me when I was finally dressed in my orange jumpsuit and waiting to see the judge. I had been listening to the other women in my pod talk about why they were in jail and every single one had a story that included addiction. Even the ones who weren't there on alcohol or drug charges were locked up because of trauma, dysfunction, violence or theft—directly resulting from addiction. The only difference between me and them was that I had been clean and working a program for a minute. I saw very clearly that I didn't deserve special treatment, that I wasn't a mystical being immune to consequences. I knew this is where my life would end up if I continued to drink and use drugs.

I also knew deep in my soul that I did not belong there. I made a decision that day to never go back.

Over the years, I found I needed more than just the 12 steps of NA to stay clean and grow up. I've tried a bunch of stuff—some has stuck, some has not. After almost a decade in recovery, I finally went to therapy to work out specific issues that I felt couldn't be fully addressed by the steps. I have continued to experience other fellowships, work with therapists, doctors and healers, as needed, to handle life's upsets and turmoil. I take full responsibility for my spiritual condition today. I know there are no quick fixes and sometimes the most meaningful lessons are learned through trial and error.

There's always a little voice in my head that says "more, more, more." That's still how addiction manifests in my life today—it's just not about the drugs and alcohol anymore. It's about the shopping, Twitter, making lists, Netflix, food, helicopter parenting, all that shit. I have to stay vigilant because I can make anything a problem, even things that are necessary or start out harmless. Long-term recovery means no matter what's going on in my life, I must make sure I get time by myself to meditate and stay connected to who I am and what I need.

I know it sounds like a big cliché but everything in my

life is because of recovery. After I got clean, I found opportunities that I would have never had otherwise. I was able to go back to school, get a couple degrees, build a career, meet a great guy, not fuck it up, get married and have an awesome kid. What I learned in my early recovery built the foundation for my future. I think I'm actually more motivated to have a happy, healthy life because of who I *used* to be.

I never thought I deserved this type of life before I got clean. I didn't dare picture myself getting old, being a mom, a wife or somebody's best friend forever. It's a cosmic joke that, as I have grown up in recovery, I've discovered why adults are so often assholes. Being a responsible member of society is really fucking hard.

There's a part of me that is still quietly blown away that I can remember to pay my mortgage on time. I'm shocked that I don't throat punch the kid who forgot my extra ice at Starbucks or throw a chair at the bitch who voted against me at the Parent Council meeting. I need recovery more than ever because and I still have the instinct to *fuck shit up*—to sabotage myself. I need the principles I learned in the steps and the support of my people to successfully navigate this life I have built.

Recovery is possible. We all deserve to really live—not just exist. The worst thing that can happen is you will fail. But addicts are awesome at failing up.

My life is proof of that.

Reclaiming Your Grace

Jennifer Lovely

I used to think it was my fault that my sons became heroin and meth addicts.

I thought I had done something wrong. I thought I was a bad mom. I was filled with guilt and shame.

I spent a lot of time going back through the past, trying to pinpoint how I had failed them. Joe and Jake grew up privileged. They went to private schools. They'd played every sport. They'd shown so much promise.

How had this happened? And how could I help them change?

Until I realized that the change had to come from within me, nothing changed. Their addictions consumed my life.

———

On Jake's 16th birthday, I dropped him off at his first rehab. He needed help.

I didn't think I needed help, but I showed up for the family recovery, Al Anon and Codependent Anonymous meetings anyway. I did everything the rehab advised. It took me four months to realize that the people in those meetings were my people. I got a sponsor in CoDA, which is what we call Codependents Anonymous. I got a therapist. I started my work.

Meanwhile, Jake left rehab, relapsed and went to another rehab. And another. And another. He couldn't stay sober. Joe and Jake's father had told me for years that their problems were because of me. I thought, let me take "the problem" out of the equation.

After his fourth rehab and the demise of my marriage, I decided to move from Orange County, California, to Washington state, where my soon-to-be ex-husband and I had a second home.

"If you aren't going to be married to me," he said, "you can't live there." So, after a few months, I moved to a small island off the coast and started over. I was 41 years old.

On the island, I remained actively involved in my recovery work. I did the steps. I was committed to healing myself. Every month, I flew down to Orange County to find my kids wherever they were living at the time. Sometimes they were homeless, sometimes they were with friends, sometimes they were with their dad. Sometimes they felt they could be sober, sometimes they didn't. I never knew what to expect.

During a two-week trip to Italy in September of 2016, Jake called to tell me he was super high on meth. It was raining and he was homeless and his brother had just betrayed him.

"And I just beat the shit out of him," he said.

Afraid he'd be arrested, I called his dad. "You need to go find him. He's in trouble. We need to get him off the streets."

The thought of my kids in jail was my worst fear.

In December of 2016, Joe, who'd been living in his car for a month, called to tell me he was going to jail. He'd been arrested for selling heroin to an underage girl.

After 10 days, I bailed him out and he went directly to rehab.

Meanwhile, Jake had driven his car off an overpass on the 405 freeway and landed in a ditch. This was the second of six major car wrecks he would have. Every accident was this disastrous—driving a car over the side of a freeway overpass, totaling a car. Every time, I couldn't believe he had survived.

In rehab, Joe found a sponsor who was super rigid and all about the principles. He found friendship and support. I thought he was in a good place.

Jake was not. He was angry, totaling cars, using meth and heroin, getting a new job, getting fired and then doing it all over again. He went to five more rehabs. He either got kicked out or ran away from each one. His life was reaching new levels of chaos.

And my life, as a result, felt chaotic.

I wasn't using drugs, but I might as well have been. My kids' addictions were my addiction. Their pain was my pain. I thought I needed to be in as much pain as them. Maybe I thought it wouldn't be fair to be happy.

Still, I tried. I bought a yoga studio in the hopes of creating a community on an island where I didn't know anyone. *I don't know why I'm doing this*, I thought, but I did it anyway. I was trying to build a new life. I knew enough about enmeshment to know I needed distance, but I still flew down to see them every month. How could I not? I was vacillating between wanting to save them and wanting to save myself.

———

In October of 2017, Jake was arrested for breaking and entering. He stayed in jail for 45 days. I didn't bail him out. I sent an attorney, who went to see Jake wearing a pink shirt and a hot pink tie.

Jake said, "You look gay. I don't want you representing me."

"He needs to stay in there a lot longer," the attorney said. "And I won't represent someone who's so disrespectful."

So Jake stayed in jail. On Thanksgiving, he called to tell me "some shit was about to go down" and he was going to "get his ass kicked." I was devastated. I was miserable in my own skin.

Finally, 45 long days later, Jake got out and went to a new rehab in San Diego. This was his 15th rehab. Sixty days in, he got kicked out. And then something really crazy happened. He moved into a new sober living and stopped using.

Joe had finished rehab and started working there.

Things were going well for Joe until he was fired for smoking pot. He didn't tell me, but he did stop calling, which was always a bad sign.

The next time I flew down, Joe was so thin that his cheekbones were jutting out. He'd lost probably 20 pounds. "I'm using again," he said. "I've been eating at soup kitchens. I don't have a job."

During this trip, I took both kids to a Mexican restaurant and sobbed the entire time, saying, "I can't keep doing this."

"It's going to be okay, Momma," they said.

But it wasn't.

Joe got popped for not completing his community service and went back to jail. In a way, it was a relief this time. Joe was good at making friends in jail; he knew how to protect himself.

One day, I went to visit him. He came to the window, super light and joyful as always. Even on heroin, he was like that.

"The phone will hang up if we stop talking," he explained. And then, during a pause in the conversation, it did. Even now, I want to cry when I think about how we put our hands on the plexiglass and mouthed, *I love you.*

———

A short time after I'd moved to the island, Jake came up for a visit. He tore like a tornado through my small town. He stole, bought drugs and hitchhiked. I brought him to a therapist who thought she could help. Jake went to a few sessions. Then one day he didn't show. The therapist called me. I told her Jake had left town and that I'd take the appointment.

"I think I need help," I said.

In this first meeting, the therapist said, "Your parts are all over the place. Would you be willing to give me six months? I promise this will be the last therapy you'll ever have to do for your trauma."

This therapist made good on her promise. She changed my life.

A lot of healing had happened for me in 12-step programs. Even more healing happened with this therapist.

Parts Therapy, as it was called, consisted of me going back to the age of five and then, year by year, learning to separate my traumatized child self from the adult I was now. By examining and honoring my past, I was able to let go of the idea that I was a victim and extract myself from my kids' addictions.

———

Joe and Jake are now in recovery. They both work in construction at the same company and they're the best of friends. Jake just had a baby with the love of his life— which means I'm a grandma.

Eventually, I sold the yoga studio and became an Onto-logical coach. I now work with individuals and families, helping them heal and find their freedom.

I teach a course called Reclaiming Your Grace, because that's what I did. Babies come into this world innocent and pure and joyful. As kids and then as adults, many of us lose ourselves to our family's generational trauma. Ultimately, what we're all trying to do is get back to our original joy. When we can find freedom for ourselves, our children are more likely to find it, too.

I've learned that most people get stuck at victimization. Being the victim is a comfortable identity and it's hard to break loose. It wasn't until I took a serious inventory of myself and claimed my part that I could drop the shame and become responsible, which is the opposite of being the victim.

Who were you? Who are you? What do you know deep down inside? How can you allow yourself to create some-thing new?

I've learned that change is possible when you truly want to change.

I've learned that you can be free.

Surviving Heroin and Homophobia

Ryan Hampton

At the peak of my heroin use in 2014, everyone knew something was wrong. My track marks, broken veins, pinpoint pupils and sunken cheeks told the whole world that I had a problem. My illness was obvious. What they didn't know was my secret: I was gay, too.

By the time I reached my bottom, I had slowly come to terms with my identity as a gay man. My mother and sisters knew. I was beginning to get comfortable with my sexual identity. I was even beginning—very cautiously—to see other men. I had one foot out of the closet. But I was still injecting heroin multiple times a day.

My addiction consumed me, making me into a shadow of my former self. An estimated 20 to 30 percent of the LGBTQ community misuses substances, compared to about nine percent of the population as a whole. I was no exception. The double stigma of homosexuality and addiction made it hard to find help. Who could I open up to? The people who accepted my identity rejected my substance use disorder, and the people who accepted my health issue rejected my identity. I was ashamed of myself, which only drove me deeper into my addiction. I felt stuck, and it was killing me.

Nobody seemed to care except my family. I couldn't keep a job and bounced from couch to couch in Los Angeles, sleeping wherever I could. I used in public bathrooms and nodded off next to the toilet until someone rattled the door. I dragged my belongings around in a black plastic garbage bag. I ate at the homeless shelter, limp sandwiches that I could hardly choke down. I barely felt human. Yet, my identity was there, even when I was completely checked out. I wish I could say that, at the bottom of my addiction, *who* I was didn't matter.

Even in California, in a city where it was relatively safe to be out as a gay person, there was only one LGBTQ rehab available to me. Most of the programs were private-pay only, which meant they cost tens of thousands of dollars per month—completely inaccessible to someone like me who relied on public assistance. The only public program that openly served the LGBTQ population was booked solid.

Other public programs said they were queer-friendly, but I knew that wasn't true; about 70 percent of the addiction treatment services that supposedly specialized in LGBTQ people were really no different from those provided to heterosexuals. The one LGBTQ rehab I found was a good one, and I went there almost every day for their 12-step meetings, begging for help.

"Please," I pleaded with the receptionist. "I just need a few weeks of treatment. I won't even take up a whole 30 days."

The program director, a gay man who was supportive and compassionate toward me, came behind the desk. "Let me see what we can do for you," he said.

My heart lifted. Maybe he'd be able to get me a bed,

maybe there was space in their program for me. Maybe, this time, I'd find help in a place that really understood me.

He pulled a hefty, three-ring binder out of a filing cabinet and laid it on the desk with a thump. It was thicker than a Bible. Loose papers protruded from its edges. The black plastic edges cracked with wear. The director flipped it open, slowly turning one laminated page after another. Some of the pages were crumpled, as though they'd been through the wash. When he got to the very back, he clicked the button on his ballpoint pen.

"Give me your phone number and we'll call you as soon as something is available," he said.

"When will that be?" I asked. My eyes were burning.

"Hard to say," he said. He wrote my name down. "When we have an open bed, we start calling these numbers, in the order they're in. When somebody answers, we offer them the bed. If they say yes, it's filled. If they say no, we call until we find a person who is ready for treatment."

I eyed the binder. "There are hundreds of names before mine," I said. "I could be dead tomorrow. I don't have time to wait for help."

He sighed and put the pen to the paper. "I know, Ryan. We're doing what we can. Give me your number and keep coming to the meetings."

Keeping a phone was a challenge, but I did it. I waited for that call every day, even when I was jiggling a syringe into my arm. I told myself that all I had to do was *not die*.

Through sheer luck, I did survive long enough to get into treatment. But after a few days, I was transferred to a different program—a program that wasn't explicitly LGBTQ friendly. I'd had one toe out of the closet, and when I was transferred, I went right back in and shut that closet door—again. I instinctively understood that if I was going to survive, stay healthy and make it into recovery, I couldn't be gay, too. Nobody could know.

The new program was divided by gender: girls and guys. It was like middle school, with teasing, flirting, scheming, and gossip passed between our separate dorms. I was the only gay person there. Even the counselors were straight. If I came out, I knew I risked being ostracized or bullied, treated like a sexual deviant, or being made to feel like an outsider. I couldn't risk that. Instead, I kept my mouth shut and pretended to get it when the other guys would talk about which female client they were going to hook up with, or how hot some movie star was. I knew better than to put my two cents in: one comment about Jennifer Lopez's nice eyes or Angelina Jolie's commitment to humanitarian aid would give me away. I was a man, but I wasn't a straight man.

Hiding nearly caused me to relapse. Keeping a secret about myself, especially something of that magnitude, made me sick with anxiety. It was like walking around with a gut full of hardboiled eggs. I was terrified that some gesture or word would give me away. Finally, when it was time to start one-on-one counseling, my mom called me.

"Son, you have to tell them," she said.

She didn't need to say *what*. We both knew.

My first counseling session, I could barely sit in the chair. My legs twitched, and I must have looked like I was on amphetamines.

"Everything okay?" the counselor asked.

I picked at the back of my neck. "I'm fine," I said.

She shrugged and looked down at my intake forms, trying to assess where to begin.

"Actually, I'm not okay," I blurted out. "I'm gay."

Those two words—*I'm gay*—were the keys to my freedom.

The counselor just nodded. She didn't mark it in my chart or ask me why I hadn't said anything before. We proceeded, working together a few times a week. Feeling accepted and knowing that my identity was acknowledged made it possible for me to open up in counseling. I finally started sharing about the sexual trauma I'd endured as a very young person, my fear that I would never be able to openly date and my worry that I would be excluded from the recovery community. I talked through those things, and though I didn't come out to anyone else in treatment, that one admission was enough to break the ice.

I stayed mostly closeted for the next couple of years. I also stayed sober, transferring to a residential sober living that supported my recovery. My best friend Garrett knew, and while some guys teased us for being "boyfriends," it was playful. We were inseparable, and enough of our female friends came over to visit that we could laugh off the insult.

Because to almost everyone "gay" was less-than. It was a way to put others down. And even those passing "just a joke" comments hurt me and made it harder for me to trust that I belonged in the recovery community.

However, time passed, and the stronger I felt about my recovery, the more confident I felt about the rest of my identity too. It took almost four years to say the words, "I'm a proud gay man in recovery." But I did say them, and when I did, I knew I was finally healing from both my addiction and the trauma of my past. I wasn't hiding anymore. I was out as a person in recovery and out as a gay man. If people didn't like it, well, that was their problem—not mine.

Coming out in recovery was one of the scariest things

I've ever done, and the best things too. I was willing to speak up and share my truth, even though it meant risking the community connections that kept me alive. Showing up for my recovery with *all* of me saved my life. It also introduced me to the love of my life, Sean, who I am marrying this November.

My only regret is that I felt I had to hide myself in order to save my own life.

Stigma, homophobia and intolerance are still very real issues in the recovery community, both in treatment centers and in the support systems that help people get healthy again. I wonder how many gay men, unable or unwilling to stay closeted, were kicked out of the same program that I went to; how many of them left because they couldn't stand being bullied or threatened by the other residents?

How many trans women were unable to find a treatment center that accepted them and offered trans-specific services and counseling? The odds are bleak for those of us who are already outsiders in a homophobic, intolerant society. My white privilege helped me keep one foot in the door, but that shouldn't be a requirement to access life-saving care.

I know how lucky I am to have survived addiction; adding my identity to the mix makes me feel like I dodged lightning. Life on the other side of treatment, with years of recovery under my belt, is better than I could ever have imagined. I wish I hadn't waited so long to have this experience.

I wish for others, who are like me and struggling to find their place in recovery, to know that they don't belong in the closet either. The answer isn't hiding; the answer is building a system that includes *all* of us. Every person who asks for help should have it, regardless of their identity or orientation, race, gender or expression.

Navigating recovery is hard enough. When I brought my *whole* self to the table, I left the closet behind. I'm holding the door open for others, too—because nobody should have to compromise themselves or hide in order to save their life.

When The Pink Cloud Wears Off

Emily Lynn Paulson

"I don't know how to do this!"

With the iconic space needle behind me, lit up with blue and green Seahawk-themed colors, I stomped my feet and cried to my husband. This was the perfect backdrop for an emotional meltdown, I thought. I couldn't have scripted a more stereotypical Seattle scene. Cold raindrops mixed with the warm, salty tears racing down my face.

Six weeks in, the infamous "pink cloud" of sobriety had worn off. The "pink cloud" can be described as a euphoric feeling in early sobriety. Some experience it for a few days, weeks or months, and others don't experience it at all. I discovered on a cold February evening that my euphoria was coming to an end. After attempting to have a 'normal' night out with friends, I was triggered, pissed off and future tripping.

"What can I do?" my kind husband asked me, getting more drenched by the minute. He walked me to my car after my "normal" night turned into an epic failure.

"I don't know. I don't want to ask you to be sober. I

don't want to collect new friends. But I know I can't do *this*. I'm not one of you anymore."

This was a birthday party for a friend at a crowded bar. Sure, bars aren't the best place for the newly sober, but having conquered a few social events in the previous few weeks, I assumed it would be fine.

And it was, for a while.

The evening began with music; me with my sparkling drink, and everyone else with their beer. I was hopeful. Calm. Happy. However, as the night continued, and everyone else carried on, getting more and more tipsy, I got annoyed. I wasn't annoyed with any one person in particular, or even the collective group of people. I was irritated at my awareness of everyone else. Why hadn't the obsession left me? I couldn't help but notice what other people were drinking, and how much they were consuming. Some were getting drunker than others. Did they have an issue with booze, too? Perhaps I'd see them in a meeting some day. I wondered if they enjoyed the taste or if they just drank it for effect like I did.

As I was engaging in my own internal dialogue, the line of questioning started. I was so sick of questions. The goddamn sober interview. It goes something like this:

"Are you still doing that thing?"

"Oh you're quitting, like, forever?"

"So you had, like, a *problem*, then?"

The inquiries, no matter how well meaning, dug into my skin like a knife.

I am not quite sure what I expected. I knew when I declared my new alcohol-free lifestyle, my life would have to change, but I didn't know how. How does one integrate their new self into their old life? Is it even possible? And if so, is that what I wanted? I'm allergic to bees and I have no interest in racing through an apiary. Why would I want to hang out with a bunch of drinkers anyway? What kind of masochist was I?

Yet I saw my husband having so much fun, in the crowd with everyone else, and there I was, standing on the sidelines. At that point, I still believed that I was missing out. I believed that I was afflicted with a spiritual, mental, physical and emotional malady that made me incapable of drinking. Cursed, even. I *couldn't* drink. *Could not*. Prohibited. Banned.

In the past, telling me that I *couldn't* do something was an open invitation to desire *that thing* even more. And there I was, surrounding myself with people doing the thing I *couldn't* do. Why was I torturing myself? Of course they had no idea what to say. What would I say to someone who was putting herself in this position? Yes, this was, in fact, the death sentence I'd worried it would be. I knew it. I thought, *I may as well collect a bunch of cats and say goodbye to my social life.*

Finally, what felt like the millionth time a friend grabbed my hand and tried to drag me on the dance floor, I lost my shit and stormed out.

I was so perplexed. How had the novelty of my sobriety worn off for most of my friends? Just six weeks earlier, I'd sent out this text:

> *Putting this out in the universe. Deep stuff on a Sunday afternoon!* 😊 *Deep breath....*
>
> *Hi, I'm Emily and I'm an alcoholic. For reals.*
>
> *I went to an AA meeting last week and I'm going again today, and will probably be going for the rest of my life.*
>
> *Some of you know I've been struggling for a long time, and some of you probably had no idea. So here it is!*
>
> *I'm done pretending that alcohol is not a problem for me. It has been the catalyst behind the continuous and progressive destruction*

of my friendships, my marriage, my health and my life, just to name a few. I am done hiding it, rationalizing it, making excuses about it and denying it.

Why am I telling you this? Because you are my friends, and I need the love and support you've always given me more than ever!

This isn't meant to be a secret or an exclusive list by any means—so feel free to share (discreetly, of course, out of earshot of kiddos).

Thank you for being there for me through all of these ups and downs, and God willing there won't be as many "downs" in 2017.

That declaration of sobriety was met with cheers, kudos, hugs and love. Friends and family who'd watched my descent to rock bottom with health problems and DUI arrests, others who I'd hid my drinking from and everyone in between were all cheering me on and wishing me well.

Yet that night my pink cloud evaporated, I was standing by my car at 10 pm, wishing things could somehow be different. Wishing I could be different. Wishing simultaneously that other people understood what it was like to be me, while also thanking God that they didn't have to endure what I had. Less than two months after shouting my alcohol-free lifestyle from the rooftops, people just seemed annoyed with me. I was annoyed with me.

My husband hugged me, both of us drenched from the rain, not knowing what to say, and he suggested I go home and call my sponsor. I was already hanging on my sponsor's every word. I was so glad I'd taken her advice to drive my own car that evening. On the way home, I called her and downloaded the events of the party—as if I was the first drunk to feel left out.

I could hear her smiling through the phone. "Nothing

is permanent," she said. "Just because you feel this way now, doesn't mean you'll feel this way forever."

"Have you ever had a bad boyfriend?" she asked.

Well shit, of course, but we hadn't quite gotten to that step, yet. She'd hear all about that later.

"Yeah, many," I offered.

"My point," she continued, "is to not be mad at yourself for missing something even if you know it's toxic. It's like missing a shitty boyfriend. There were still some good times, even during the shit."

It was oddly comforting. I understood. I had to mourn the loss of booze. It had ruined my life, but the romanticized version I created in my mind needed to be mourned.

"It's like a breakup," she added. "Or even a death. You need to get through every season."

With that suggestion, 2017 became the year of mourning. By the time 2018 rolled around, I realized that she was 100 percent correct.

———

At the end of 2019, I was leaving a television studio after doing an interview about my book. Once again, I was standing in front of the iconic Space Needle. Just short of three years later, in the exact same setting, there were so many differences. There was no shame in my life, or in my recovery. There was no desire to be "normal" and in fact no desire to understand what "normal" actually was. Normal doesn't exist.

The greatest lesson I've learned is that recovery isn't one size fits all. I no longer view alcohol as something I can't have, but rather as a substance that adds nothing to my life. I no longer believe that I lack willpower or control, but rather that I've gathered skills to gain control of my own life, my own feelings and my own experience. The powerful realization brought tears to my eyes and I felt the distinct contrast of cold rain on my face, once again.

I'm so grateful for that year of mourning.

And I really need to get an umbrella.

Nineteen-And-A-Half

Patrick O'Neil

It's 7:53 at night and I'm sitting in front of the computer as another online AA meeting winds down. On the monitor, screen rows of addicts and alcoholics stare into their cameras or off into space. A few are petting cats, a couple on a lumpy couch is stuffing food in their faces and one old man is clearly taking a snooze. The woman that shares every week about the same problem is yakking away, even after the timer has signaled for her to stop.

"I acknowledge you," she says, waving off the young woman holding up her phone to the camera as the timer sounds.

I roll my eyes. Why is it so hard to adhere to the concept of a three-minute share? And why does it bother me so much when a recovering drunk can't follow the rules? Not like I ever did.

I've been going to meetings for a long time. Well, to me it's a long time. I have more than 19 years free from drugs and alcohol and I can safely say no one ever saw that coming. What with the way I had been living and destroying everything I touched, it didn't take a fortuneteller to know I wasn't heading down the primrose path to a wonderful productive life. Shooting heroin since I was 17, I was what behavioral sociologists label a "career junkie." But that only scratched the surface. I was also a bank robber, a useless boyfriend, an absent family member, a self-centered egotist with low self-esteem and definitely not the person you'd call in a time of need.

My addiction was all consuming and I saw no way out. I had a habit that a normal workingman's salary couldn't support—not that I had ever held an actual job, normal or otherwise. I tried dealing drugs to pay for my habit but I ended up using them all. Eventually I turned to armed robbery. The summer of '97, the cops kicked in my front door and dragged me off to jail. I was charged with multiple felonies and held on a million-dollar bail. The DA decided to throw the proverbial book at me and I was looking at 25 years to life in prison. With the help of a pricey lawyer, I eventually plead out to two strikes, did my time and got out on parole.

———

The secretary thanks the woman, politely cutting her off. "That's all the time we have for sharing. Does anyone have a burning desire, meaning they may drink tonight?"

The silence in my room at home is deafening. In a live meeting, the kind we used to hold just three months ago, that silence meant everyone's sobriety was pretty much intact. But on Zoom it just feels weirdly desperate. Like no one is really admitting this pandemic is scaring the shit out of all of us and the thought of getting loaded has probably crossed everyone's mind—even if it's just a fleeting "I don't want to feel like this right now."

The secretary hands the meeting over to the chip

person. Although this meeting is virtual and the closest anyone will get to a chip is seeing it dangling in front of the camera.

———

A week after the New Year in 2001, I walked into a long-term residential rehab. My only intention was to stay one step ahead of my parole officer. As a convicted felon, I was on what's known as high control parole, which basically means I was under heavy scrutiny with constant surveillance, unannounced piss tests, parole agents showing up at my work and home whenever they pleased and mandatory weekly appointments reporting live and in person.

With this kind of "supervision," one would think I would have walked the straight and narrow—at least until I was discharged—especially with the ever-present threat of going back to prison for life. Yet this exact disregard for myself, and my wellbeing, was a true testament to the pull of heroin addiction. Regardless of these very real conse-quences, I had stopped checking in (technically called absconding) and was again shooting dope and committing petty crimes to support my habit. It was only a matter of time before I was caught and sent back to prison.

The counselor doing intake took one look at me, told me the rehab was full and that I should come back the next week when there would be an opening. Not that willing to actually quit heroin, I took this as a sign I was free to use all weekend and return on Monday to be saved. Screw those bastards at parole. Checking myself into rehab was a get out of jail free card. I'd be in treatment before they found me, and by then it'd be old news and they'd just let me stay rather than deal with the hassle of violating me.

With the entire weekend open and available, I was going to shoot dope until I was really ready to quit. The counselor's words were like a reprieve from hell and I was out the door and around the block just about to call my dealer. Then my phone rang. It was the counselor I had just left. He had pulled some strings. There was an available bed. I should come back immediately. Reluctantly I returned, and the rest, as they say, is history.

———

I know the chip person. He's wrapped really tight. One of those alcoholics that's a stickler for rules and if there's the slightest change to anything, his "serenity" falls apart.

"Is anyone celebrating an anniversary? Meaning you've remained sober for a year or more? A year is 365 days. So no increments of less than a year, *please!*"

A youngster wearing a backward baseball cap waves his hand and the chip person calls on him. "Bobby, alcoholic…I have a year," he timidly whispers.

A dozen hands wave congratulations on the screen, the couple on the couch continues eating and the old man is still asleep.

"Anyone else?" The chip person's beady eyes scan the sea of little rectangles that frame all our faces.

I lean into my computer and unmute myself, "I have 19-and-a-half years."

The chip person's face turns bright red and his eyes bug out. "You're not supposed to…I said only years, goddamn it!"

I suppress a giggle and exit the meeting.

These past 19 (and a half) years have been a long worthwhile journey. Not always easy, at times incredibly hard and others immensely rewarding. I have never regretted making the decision to ask for help, enter rehab, get clean and stay clean. I'm grateful to have an amazing supportive group of people in my life. I continue to have a healthy relationship with a cool-ass sponsor who only has my best interest at heart. I socialize with fellow addicts and alcoholics and attend meetings as an integral member of the recovery community. Whenever possible I give back by being of service to others.

And yet even with all that "recovery" the old irreverent me still resurfaces now and then. You could say I'm a work in progress.

After the Crisis

Victoria English Martin

The first crisis was the death of my mother.

After the attorney revealed that she had left me nothing in her will, my grandmother turned to me and said, "Now you know what she really thought of you."

Like many people, I grew up in a dysfunctional family heavily influenced by addiction and mental illness. My mother was frighteningly unstable and without resources. My dad battled with his own drinking, but thankfully stopped when I was 14 and switched to running marathons instead. My brother has struggled with addiction his whole life. In this dynamic, I was the fixer, the one who tried to make everyone happy. I was also the one who could drink normally—or so I thought.

I went to a big football school and was in a sorority. I definitely drank, but never too much. I married a year out of college and immediately had three children within four years. During that time, I can count on one hand the number of times I drank more than two glasses of wine. I thought I'd dodged a bullet. I never gave addiction a second thought until my mother died. I was 29 years old.

After that meeting with the attorney, I flew home alone. During the flight and at the airport when we landed, I drank. A lot. I got so drunk that I had to ask the cabbie to pull over so I could vomit. When I got into bed, my husband said, "How are you?"

I said, "I think I'm broken."

That was the beginning.

It would take me almost 20 years to get one straight year of sobriety.

————

After my mom died, I started having anxiety attacks, but I didn't know what they were. I just knew I couldn't breathe. I went from easily running five or six miles a day to not being able to run even one. In an attempt to catch my breath and quiet the noise in my head, I turned to wine. Yes, wine would help me breathe more easily.

The next thing I knew, I was opening a bottle of wine by myself. Then I was hiding the bottle of wine I'd opened myself and opening a new one with my husband and pouring a glass as if it was my first.

"Boy," my husband said, "you're drinking more than you used to."

He was right.

So I stopped.

One day I tried to explain to my husband how broken I felt. I wasn't the daughter my mother had wanted me to be. I was a disappointment. Desperate for reassurance, I said, "I need you to promise you won't ever make me feel that way."

"I'll try," he said.

"No, I need you to promise."

"I'll try," he said again.

A year later he left.

And the wine came back.

I was still holding together a functional life. I took the kids to school, taught Pilates out of my home studio, picked the kids up, taught more, drank and went to bed. Alcohol had become a habit, but I knew I wasn't as bad as my brother or as bad as those drunk moms you see in movies who are unable to care for their kids. I was a good mother, I was running my own business, I was doing well.

Four years after my divorce, I remarried and had a daughter. The second I was done nursing her, my drinking took off in a new way. One morning before taking her out for a run, I looked at the liquor cabinet and thought, *I want a drink.* It was 10 am.

This scared me enough to try some moderation. I wouldn't drink vodka. I would only drink on Fridays. I would only drink beer. How, I wondered, could I be so disciplined in my life but not be able to control this one thing?

AA helped me string together bits of sobriety, but I felt like a failure for not doing the program perfectly so I self-sabotaged. The night before I was supposed to take a chip, I would drink and feel like even more of a failure. I had no compassion for myself. I was trying so hard to stay sober, but I kept ending up in a black out.

When I had my three older kids in the 90s, mommy wine culture hadn't really come into style. By the time I had my fourth kid in the 2000s it was in full swing, which made it much easier to justify my drinking. All the other moms were drinking at soccer practice and at the park, talking about the stresses of their lives. It reinforced the message I so desperately wanted to believe: my drinking wasn't *that* bad.

After my teenagers graduated from high school and I

was no longer legally entangled with their father, we moved from Miami to Denver. There, I hung onto longer periods of sobriety, but when I went back to drinking, it was worse —much worse. Instead of moderating for weeks, I could only go days. And when I picked up a drink, I lost control over what happened.

I went back to AA and did the same dance I'd done before. I held myself up to an impossible standard and hated myself for not being able to meet it. My son had gotten sober after using drugs in high school but kept relapsing. My daughter was hospitalized for bipolar disorder. And my other daughter was violently attacked in college. I couldn't tolerate the stress. And so, I drank.

In 2018, I'd strung together a good length of sobriety and my life was in a decent place. My daughter had gone through the trial for her attack, my other daughter was fairly stable and about to graduate from college and my son was sober again and thriving.

Then the second crisis happened.

———

"You got the clusterfuck of breast cancer," was how my doctor put it. The official diagnosis was triple negative breast cancer, an extremely rare and aggressive type.

Now that I was in for the fight of my life, I thought I would surely never want to drink again. All my goals would be focused on health. I considered my alcohol problem to be solved permanently so I prepared to do anything to beat cancer.

A ton of poison was pumped into my body. I underwent 16 rounds of chemotherapy, 28 rounds of radiation, a double mastectomy, a full hysterectomy and six months of oral chemo like a champ. Just as I'd done with AA and with my mother, I decided I was going to be perfect. I was going to be the best breast cancer patient ever. I made a promise to my oncologist to do 30 push-ups on my last day of treatment. Despite the fact that I was painfully thin, had no eyebrows and was bald as a cue ball, I did it.

I thought that if I did everything perfectly, I would be cancer free.

Then I went in for my double mastectomy and found out that not all of the cancer was gone. They removed it, but I remained at a high risk for recurrence. I considered myself a failure.

Feeling inadequate because I hadn't beat the cancer was devastating. So was living with the physical and emotional side effects. Eventually, I went back to drinking. Because my body was compromised, alcohol took a rapid toll. The thoughts in my head were dismal: *I'm not good enough, I can't do anything perfectly, I can't fix cancer, I couldn't get justice for my daughter after she was victimized or change my mother's opinion of me—so I'm just going to destroy myself.*

During a trip to see my kids in Florida, I wanted to die. I had scars where I'd once had breasts and an inch or two of post-chemo hair. I felt like it had all been a waste. I'd beaten cancer only to drown myself in alcohol.

I looked down at Miami Beach from my top floor hotel balcony. As I thought about lifting my leg over the railing, the faces of my children came into my mind. No, this can't be how it ends, I thought. I hated myself, but I loved them. I quickly ran into the bathroom and locked myself in so that I couldn't see the balcony anymore.

This, my lowest point, was what finally allowed me to get help.

I found a psychotherapist, an addiction psychiatrist and a breast cancer specialist. I started EMDR. I went back to AA. I read a lot. I was inspired by the stories of women who'd stopped trying to fix everybody else and instead focused on bettering their own lives.

———

When I had cancer, my pain was visible. I was frail. I had no hair. After I recovered, my hair came back and I was smiling and hiking, but inside I was unhappier than I had ever been.

We hear a lot of stories about people battling through difficult times. The end of these stories is: *They made it!*

But what happens after that moment of victory? How *do* we walk through the world after a crisis? How often are we pretending we're okay when we're not? What about the invisible pain on the inside?

These questions led to the creation of my podcast, *After the Crisis*. I interview women who have struggled with all sort of things, including infertility, addiction and domestic abuse. My hope is to broaden the scope of how we view disaster and pain and to give these survivors a place to be honest without judgment.

If cancer or alcohol had taken me out, I would have missed the chance to hear these women's stories. I would have missed the opportunity to help other people through my coaching practice. I would have missed the chance to live an authentic life.

Somebody asked me once, "Why did you fight so hard against cancer?"

"For my family," I said. I didn't give a damn about myself.

Ironically, it took cancer and nearly killing myself after cancer to finally find some compassion for myself. That little seed of compassion grew and has blossomed into what it is today. I care about myself enough not to drink.

I've also found compassion for my mother.

She was a woman suffering with mental illness during a time when there weren't many resources beyond, "Take a valium." Just like alcohol made me behave in ways that were not authentic to who I really am, her mental illness did the same to her. I know that if my mother could have done better, she would have.

California Anonymous

Lisa Smith

In the fall of 2019, after nearly 30 years of law firm life in New York City, I moved to California and launched my own business. My husband and I decided to make a beach town north of San Diego our new home, lured by the prospect of year-round sunshine and a slower pace of life. I had been ready to hang up my pavement-pounding winter boots for a long time. And if I never again had to squeeze my way onto a D train overflowing with sweaty Yankees fans on their way to a game, even better. Despite the weepy goodbyes, I took comfort in knowing I'd be back frequently. The anticipation of smelling flowers when I walked outside in the morning instead of smelling, well, New York City, had me counting down the days.

Even with 15 sober years under my belt, I knew that embarking on a top-to-bottom new life across the country would challenge my recovery. I'd be a stranger in a new town and alone until my husband joined me in a month or so. When I combined those facts with the number of bars and restaurants within walking distance from our house—most of them screaming "Happy Hour!" from their sun-drenched patios—I appreciated the fragility of my recovery. No one knew me. I could nonchalantly saunter up to a hostess, peer over my sunglasses to request a table for one, order fish tacos and say, "Sure, I'd love a cocktail with that. Dry Grey Goose martini up with a twist. Thank you!" The speed with which my mind went there was terrifying.

Of course, I could have done the same thing in New York City. I could have found a dark bar on a side street, or any street, and casually ducked in. But that city and I had done hand-to-hand combat for decades. First through my mad descent into alcohol and cocaine addiction, and then again through the hard work of halting addiction and self-destruction in order to embrace a new life. Being there had helped fuel my drinking and drugging and it eventually fueled my recovery. As the saying goes, where you find a great place to get wasted, you find a great place to get sober.

Fortunately, I had met several San Diego-area sober women through social media before my move. People in recovery share a certain unspoken understanding with each other. In the way twins have a secret language or fraternities have a secret handshake, I can say, "I'm sober, too," to a stranger, and on a gut level we understand each other. In my head, it sounds like, "Wow, you were in that war, too? That sucked. Let's stick together so we never have to go back there."

I may never have shared a cup of coffee with that person before, but in a very real way I know them, and they know me, better than most of my friends and family.

It was in search of this camaraderie that I attended a recovery meeting with those ladies at 8 am on one of my first Saturdays in California. The meeting was in the back room of a vegan restaurant that didn't even open for business for two more hours. The giant room with high ceilings, dark wood, luscious plants and a kaleidoscope of mismatched pillows strewn about didn't feel right. Most of the people in the overflowing space looked relaxed, fit, glowing and grateful to be there. They hugged and smiled and whispered to each other, decked out in board shorts, yoga pants and fuzzy UGGs, even though it was still summer.

"How is your dog doing?" a woman holding a bottle of green juice asked another.

"Good! Thank you for asking. We're going on a hike this afternoon. Do you two want to join us?" After automatically assuming the fourth party being invited was human, it occurred to me it was more likely the green juice woman's dog. Wow.

My regular Saturday morning recovery meeting in New York had been in a basement room with bad lighting, folding chairs, a draft and a somewhat cranky crowd that was headed for the diner —not the beach—afterwards. They were my people. Like most New Yorkers I knew, they spoke frankly, cursed a lot and didn't tolerate bullshit.

"It was pouring rain this morning and I almost said, 'Fuck it, I'm going back to bed,'" one friend said on more than one occasion. He'd add, "But then I reminded myself that if I could get to the liquor store in the rain, I can get to the meeting in the rain. I feel like shit today, but I'm here."

The speed at which I fell into the flow of my new surroundings in San Diego shocked me. These people knew how to enjoy life in a way I hadn't imagined. In New York, I was all business, anxiously focused on the next five things I had to do. People would ask me if I had seen any good theater lately and I would realize that I hadn't been to the theater all season. I maintained tunnel vision, whether it was to get from one end of the subway platform to the other during rush hour or staring at my phone while waiting in line to pick up my pre-ordered lunch salad from Sweetgreen.

Maybe it was an oversaturation of vitamin D, but these Southern Californians actually *appreciated* everything around them. In conversation, they held earnest eye contact, not distractedly looking over my shoulder as we spoke. I learned to do the same. They would observe their surroundings, take deep breaths and remark on what a beautiful day it was. And these were people who grew up in San Diego, surrounded by beautiful days their entire lives. New York had become wallpaper for me. California remained a joyful revelation to them.

Suddenly, when I wasn't traveling for work, I was in tea houses, vegan restaurants, hot yoga classes and working with a transformational healer. Clothing in colors other than black, white and gray started to hang in my closet. I regularly attended a recovery meeting at a women's sober living house so I could stay connected with newcomers and be of service for others. When I was home in California, it felt like half-vacation, half-restoration and the 30 years of intense urban life began to fade away.

Then came COVID-19. Like so many others, all my work travel halted. No more back and forth to the East Coast. Those monthly visits for a couple of nights with my mom in New Jersey? Gone. The feeling of deserving a break when I returned to California after two weeks of back-to-back travel? Gone. Even though I was still working and studying to become a recovery coach, my old life was gone. It was like seeing a snow globe shaken and watching helplessly as the flakes just fell haphazardly. I had no control. None of us did.

Despite the fact that my husband was with me by that point, California's stay-at-home order brought isolation, something I had assiduously avoided in recovery, into my life again. My brain bolted back in time to the Friday afternoons I would leave the office early to get home to meet my drug dealer. Once he left, I would double-bolt the door, pull all the shades and spend the weekend alone with an eight-ball of cocaine, enough cheap wine for a bachelorette party and three packs of cigarettes. The memory turns my stomach.

It wasn't just the isolation. Lockdown made me feel like I was slacking on my work and avoiding family and friends as I did when I was drinking, even though my rational mind knew it wasn't about me. It was about a pandemic unprecedented in my lifetime. How was I going to stay sober in such unfamiliar territory?

I didn't fully realize the answer until about two months into the crisis. It's the same answer it's been every time I've struggled in the past. I put one foot in front of the other. I took the next right action and let go of the results. I accepted the things I couldn't change, primarily not being able to work and see my people in New York. I changed the things I could. That meant connecting with everyone, including other sober folks, online instead of in person. It wasn't perfect, but it kept me from drifting.

I also brought to bear what I learned from my California people. I appreciated what was around me every day. Instead of getting up in the morning and feeling frustrated by what I couldn't do, I learned to treasure what I could do. I started taking long walks, tried out a slow cooker (with decidedly mixed results), limited exposure to anxiety-inducing news and reached out to help others whose difficulties far exceeded my own.

I allowed myself to feel grief at the loss of my prior life and uncertainty about the future. And I practiced radical self-care with meditation, trashy books, midday naps and bubble baths. I did not pick up a drink or a drug.

Just as it had in the early days of recovery, taking each day as it came, the true practice of "one day at a time" saved me. It still does. Just for today, I can show up and try to live in the moment, let go of what I can't control and be gentle with myself. It hasn't been perfect, and it never will be. But whatever the future brings, if I stay connected to these ideas and my precious sober people, I will be fine. In fact, I will be better than fine. I can have peace.

Flipping the Coin

Emily Redondo

When I was a teenager tagging along with my sober mother to AA speaker meetings, recovery looked easy. All you had to do was quit drinking, go to some meetings, tack up slogans all over the house and stop acting like an asshole, right? I knew the 12 steps better than my geometry homework, so it made no sense to me why my angry alcoholic father, living under the same roof, never got on board. All I knew was my house was a weekly catastrophe and when I grew up, I was going to be nothing like them.

Turns out I was much worse.

I learned everything through failure. Okay, maybe not everything, but in terms of my love/hate relationship with addiction, you'd be hard pressed to not agree with me. When I first got sober in 2002 as a single mom with a four-year-old daughter, I thought I had a Fast Pass in my pocket, a ticket to the front of the line where all the old-timers with 10-plus years of sobriety like my mother hung out. Then it was 2004, after my impressive plummet into "progressive drinking," which basically means I was chugging mouthwash and going nuts.

By the time I was happily married (for the third time) with three adorable daughters, I thought I knew everything. Both my husband and I had years of sobriety and I was a stay-at-home mom, active in my recovery, mothering the heck out of my kids in my cute neighborhood. I never wondered if I could drink in moderation or if I was somehow magically cured. I didn't think about drinking; I barely thought at all. I was so busy trying to keep up with my dream life, making sure everyone was happy and fed. Someone constantly needed me to carry them, wipe their face, wipe their butt, clean the spill, pick up toys, pack a bag, pack a snack, sit in carpool. And then, while I can't remember when it started, an uncomfortable feeling of constant pressure started to fester in the back of my mind.

I ignored it.

To talk about the brutality of addiction on a personal level is by far the most intriguing part of the story for most people who know me, because I hid everything. I can barely remember the days when I drank in front of another person and can barely remember a time when I wasn't either sober or trying to be. It's been decades since I enjoyed a drink at a bar or with friends. But beyond the intrigue of my dramatic drunk-a-logs is my gift of failure. I deserve a trophy.

Right before I entered my seventh rehab in 2016, something happened. Time was what I cried over now—how much I'd lost, how much I didn't even remember and how I didn't have much left. I was so sick of myself and so tired of fighting and failing, and I was exceptionally tired of people telling me all the things that were wrong with me.

My failures are my greatest asset, and I can't believe I'm saying that. I would have slapped someone if I'd heard those words before I was ready to see the truth in them. A mother who went to rehab seven times, found out she was pregnant with her son in a detox center, checked into multiple intensive outpatient programs and psych wards, lost her driver's license for driving drunk with a daughter in the car, plus worse, didn't deserve to have *assets*; that's crazy.

Admittedly, it took a full year of sobriety and fresh-start thinking before I embraced myself as a successful failure. Shame and remorse cut through me like the Grand Canyon and it took a lot of work to fill up the hole of pain inside me. Over the course of 14 years, I'd been given countless suggestions, opinions, tools and techniques by gurus, professionals and experts who thought they had the perfect solutions for my problems. They weren't right or wrong. They also weren't my problem; I was.

I started looking at those years of tragically bad decisions like a coin with two sides. Yes, there were awful, ugly parts and for that, I took responsible actions to clean up my messes and learn from them. I definitely didn't want to deep dive into the very pool of crap I was repeatedly getting drunk to avoid. But if I wanted to live, I had to.

Still, it was the other side of that coin that fascinated me. What if something good actually existed in me? What if I had something to offer? I didn't know yet because my old pattern of early sobriety looked something like this: my kids would be hugging me, laughing and having a great time, and all I could think about was how horrible a human I was. Or I'd replay old scenes of stupid decisions I'd made that terrified those precious little kids until my brain was ready to explode. It was those thoughts that had to go—meaning, I had to let them go.

My eyes were opened in a new way that stung for a second but were then left wide open to see the endless moments of payback, peace and fun still left in store. The flip side told me I'd served my sentence. It reminded me to embrace every minute I still have breath in my lungs. Now it was time to get a life and use it.

I'm still a stay-at-home mom, sober now for almost four years. Sometimes it sounds like a long time; it's not. Shame and remorse weren't the only things in that massive canyon, so I'll be healing for quite some time. I don't claim to be an expert about addiction, trauma, treatment, mental health, anxiety, depression, relapse or motherhood; I tend to shy away from those who do. My knowledge came from failures and it turned into wisdom. It's valuable, maybe even priceless.

I'm not a big deal on any level and don't have aspirations of fame or fortune. My house is still loud and crazy, and I still can't keep my closet clean to save my ass— which, by the way, has gone missing due to a shift in priorities. Life isn't perfect, and if it were I'd be bored out of my mind. I'm still learning new things, still failing fabulously, but most of all, I'm happy to be at peace and not dead. I used to pray my guts off for a do-over, a second chance, a ninth chance, but I thought God never heard me. Now I'm here, helping others recover—including those four kids of mine, right along with myself.

Maybe He did hear me and I'm living my do-over. Either way, I'm glad I stuck around this time.

Author Biographies

Colleen Connaughton was born and raised in Queens, New York. She earned a BA in political science from Columbia University and worked as a foreign journalist and television producer for Reuters TV for 16 years, traveling the globe to report stories. Colleen now lives on Long Island with her teenage sons and beloved pets.

Emerson Dameron (https://about.me/emersondameron) is a writer, storyteller, playwright and occasional comedian based in Los Angeles. He's performed at RISK!, Write Club LA, Drunkalogue, The Ruby, Choose Your Own Religion and elsewhere. He's written for Vox, Psymposia, Not For Tourists, Public Assembly and many other fine media. He likes to save bees from drowning in his swimming pool.

Monique Elise (https://www.girltalkandcoffee.com) is a storyteller and advocate, who empowers women to heal their trauma and transform their lives. She is the creator and writer of Girl Talk and Coffee, a platform in which stories and experiences are used to help others. Monique believes storytelling has the power to not only heal trauma and addiction but also combat societal stigma and mobilize meaningful change in how we treat addiction. You can find her on Instagram at @girltalkandcoffee and on Facebook at facebook.com/GirlTalkCoffee.

Ryan Hampton (https://www.ryanhampton.org) is a former White House staffer who has worked with multiple non-profits and national recovery advocacy campaigns. He was singled out by Forbes as a top social entrepreneur and has been featured by—and is a contributor to—media outlets such as *USA Today*, *Fox and Friends*, *The New York Times*, *The Wall Street Journal*, NPR, MSNBC, HLN, Vice, Forbes, Slate, HuffPost, The Hill and others. His first book, *American Fix — Inside the Opioid Addiction Crisis and How to End It*, published by St. Martin's Press, was released in August 2018. You can find him on Instagram at @ryanjhampton and on Facebook at facebook.com/AddictionX-America.

Tawny Lara (https://www.tawnylara.com) is an NYC-based writer who covers all things sex, sobriety and rock n roll. She's even been dubbed The Sober Sexpert. Her words have been published in Playboy, Men's Health and HuffPost. Check out her podcast, Recovery Rocks, and her blog, SobrieTeaParty.com. Fun fact: Tawny has a spicy taco dish named after her ("La Chica Diabla") in her hometown of Waco, Texas. You can find her on Instagram at @tawnymlara.

Christy Leis (https://www.christycordero.com) is an innovative creative like her mama, mother of three amazing beings, life-long dream worker, brown girl and recovering codependent who is constantly evolving. She is trained in the Compassionate Inquiry process, a psychotherapeutic approach developed by Dr. Gabor Matè. In her decade of experience as a Speech Pathologist working with children and families, she learned that every being is uniquely gifted and uniquely challenged—an insight she brings to her work today. You can find her on Instagram at @cudgie__.

Jessica Lopez (https://www.allthingsjesslopez.com) is a native to the Pacific Northwest, where she lives with her husband of 10 years and their five-year-old twins. She works from home, partnering with the #1 skincare brand in America. Passionate about empowering other women, Jessica spends much of her time helping those around her to succeed in their dreams. In her previous life, Jessica graduated with a degree in Administration of Justice and worked as a Corrections Officer and a Domestic Violence Advocate. As a survivor of domestic violence, she is a huge supporter of giving women the support and tools they need to safely escape abuse. You can find her on Instagram at @all_things_jess_lopez and on Facebook at facebook.com/allthingsjesslopez.

Jennifer Lovely (https://www.jenniferlovelycoaching.com) is an Ontological and Recovery Coach who empowers those who want to reclaim their lives back and desire to be more than what their trauma has told them they are, She loves the messy grit of life and getting her hands dirty with her clients. In addition to her Reclaiming Grace program, she works with clients on an individual basis. She also has a podcast called Wet P*ssy, which is all about living our lives from the juiciest place possible. You can find her on Instagram at @jenniferllovely and on Facebook at facebook.-com/jenniferlovelycoaching.

Sean Paul Mahoney (https://www.seanologues.com) is a writer based in Portland, Oregon. His works have appeared on The Fix, The Good Men Project and After-Party Magazine. A collection of his essays, *Now That You've Stopped Dying* was released last year and is available on Amazon. He also works as a recovery mentor, advocate and program manager for the Mental Health and Addiction Association of Oregon. His works can currently be found on Medium and his own site. You can find him on Instagram at @seanpaulmahoney and on Facebook at facebook.com/sean.p.mahoney.7.

Jacq Maren (https://www.jacqmaren.com) is a writer and recovery advocate whose work has appeared in MindBody-Green and Elephant Journal. She brings more than 20 years of marketing and business development to Girl Put a Cork In It, the anonymous and judgment-free online community for sober-curious women she owns and operates. In her advocacy, Maren promotes a health-focused perspective for women in all stages of their lives. You can find her on Instagram at @girlputacorkinit and on Facebook at facebook.com/girlputacorkinit.

Victoria English Martin (https://www.victoriaenglishmartin.com) is an author, Certified Recovery Coach, Integrative Nutritionist, Pilates instructor, breast cancer advocate and host of the podcast After the Crisis. She helps clients discover why they develop maladaptive coping skills after trauma, and leads them toward empowerment, self-advocacy and healing. You can find her on Instagram at @victoriaenglishmartin and on Facebook at facebook.com/victoria.e.martin.5.

Patrick O'Neil (https://www.patrick-oneil.com) is the author of the memoirs *Anarchy at the Circle K* (forthcoming), *Gun, Needle Spoon* (Dzanc Books, 2015), and *Hold-Up* (13e Note Editions, 2013). His writing has appeared in numerous publications including: Juxtapoz, Salon.com, The Fix, AfterParty Magazine, The Nervous Breakdown and Razorcake. Patrick is a contributing editor for Sensitive Skin Magazine, a Pushcart nominee, a two-time nominee for Best Of The Net, and a PEN Center USA Professional and former Mentor. He is honored to be on the Board of Directors for REDEEMED, a non-profit Criminal Record Clearing Project that brings lawyers and professional writers together to help others move beyond their pasts. Patrick holds an MFA from Antioch University Los Angeles where he is an adjunct faculty member for the inspiration2publication program. He also teaches creative writing at various rehabs, correctional facilities, institutions and workshops. You can find him on Instagram at @patricksoneil.

Emily Lynn Paulson (https://www.highlightreallife.com) is a certified professional recovery coach, She Recovers Designated Coach, This Naked Mind Institute Trainee, founder of Sober Mom Squad and a member of the long-term recovery community. She has appeared on media outlets including *The Doctors, Parade, Today Parents*, Bustle, and *USA Today*, discussing how to end the shame and stigma of mental health by and substance abuse disorder. The bestselling author of *Highlight Real: Finding Honesty & Recovery Beyond the Filtered Life*, Emily has been sober since January 2, 2017. She resides in Seattle with her husband and their five children. You can find her on Instagram at @highlightrealrecovery and on Facebook at facebook.com/emilylynnpaulson.

Emily Redondo (https://therealemilyredondo.com) is a 45-year-old married mother of four children ranging in age from 9 to 21 years old. She's a college graduate in psychology who was working on a master's degree in counseling and is now a stay-at-home mom and a certified writing coach. She's been published at The Fix, Genius Recovery and is a contributor to Launch Pad on Medium.com. Currently, Emily is finishing her memoir and continues to help others caught somewhere in the middle of addiction, madness and recovery. You can find her on Instagram at @emily_redondo.

Paul Roux (http://www.paulrouxcoaching.com) is a writer, life coach, formal financial advisor and recovery advocate. He believes everyone has unique gifts they can use to find meaning and bring joy and freedom to their lives. In his coaching practice, Paul works with courageous individuals who are ready to embrace their superpowers, become financially empowered and learn to "play for their dreams." You can find him on Instagram at @masterproux and on Facebook at facebook.com/paul.roux.5243.

Becky Sasso (http://www.beckyjsasso.com) is a writer and editor with more than a decade of experience in publishing, nonprofits and higher ed. She has a MA in Digital Communication from Johns Hopkins University. Her first professional writing gig was in 2008, developing recovery literature at the world headquarters of the international nonprofit Narcotics Anonymous, Inc. She has written, co-authored and edited numerous books, informational pamphlets and marketing materials. Her work can be found on rehabreviews.com, Afterparty Magazine, The Fix, In Recovery Magazine and soberinfo.com. Becky lives in the suburbs of LA with her husband, son and a cat named Bruce. You can find her on Instagram at @bookybeckyj.

Lauren Schwarzfeld (http://www.everythinglauren.com) is a writer, coach and leader in community engagement. She helps women rediscover their strengths, passion and confidence to reclaim a spot in their life as they step outside the box of perceived expectations. Her goal is for women to create a future that is authentically and unapologetically their own. You can find her on Instagram at @lschwarzfeld and on Facebook at facebook.com/lauren.schwarzfeld.

Bucky Sinister is the author of four books of poetry, two self-help books, and a science fiction novel, *Black Hole*. When he's not writing, he competes in kettlebell sport. He has been clean and sober since 2002. He lives next to the noisiest neighbors in Los Angeles. You can find him on Facebook at facebook.com/buckysinisterprofile.

Lisa Smith (https://www.lisasmithadvisory.com) is a recovery coach, writer, speaker, and podcast host, as well as a former practicing lawyer and law firm executive. She is the author of *Girl Walks Out of a Bar*, her award-winning memoir of high-functioning addiction and recovery in the world of New York City corporate law. She co-hosts the podcast, Recovery Rocks. Sober for more than 15 years, Lisa now lives in the San Diego area with her husband, Craig. You can find her on Instagram at @girlwalksout and on Facebook at facebook.com/girlwalksoutofabar.

Acknowledgments

Colleen Connaughton: To my mother, Sheila Connaughton, who never let me down.

Emerson Dameron: Thanks to Janet Quinonez of Drunkalogue, Gabi Conti and Shawn Binder of Burn Your Baggage and everyone else in the Los Angeles storytelling scene who's given me a chance to share my work in progress for rapturous audiences. Much love to Vince Horn, Jessica Graham, Recovery Dharma and the rest of you who've nurtured my lifesaving meditation practice. Special thanks to Beth Lapides for your wide-ranging support and encouragement. May you live with open hearts.

Monique Elise: There are many people who have touched my life and helped shape me into the person I am today. Together, I'd like to thank: my mother for bringing me into this world even though she was far from ready. She's given me a life full of profound lessons and an enormous amount of laughter that we, as a family, express in roaring, almighty cackles. Without her, I wouldn't be the woman I am today. She is a powerful woman—proof that we can all rise from the bowels of life.

My sisters, Chantelle and Katlyn, for their forgiveness, enduring love and support. During my worst years, I forgot how to protect them. Instead, I exposed them to my heroin use and criminal activities. In the end, they never stopped loving me. Even more, my sisters, who are seven and nine years younger than me, became my teachers. I turned to them when I struggled in school and when I wanted to learn how to write.

Ryan Preddy, my dear friend, who helped save my life. He taught me how to enter society, how to function with a job, a home and an education. He taught me how to drive. But, most importantly, he taught me how to be a true friend. He was kind, patient and generous even when I didn't deserve it. When I was stuck in survival mode and living like a selfish parasite, he still showed me compassion and care.

Anna David, the Launch Pad team and my fellow co-authors of *The Addiction Diaries*, who have all so bravely shared their stories and made this book possible. You've all given a voice that will help others and inspire powerful change in the world of addiction.

And finally, I dedicate my story and all of my work to my three darling nephews, their mother and their father, who is also my brother—my first best friend. It's my love for all of you that inspires me to want to help others and create change. Don't ever forget how much I love you.

Ryan Hampton: A special thanks to the love of my life, Sean, for keeping me centered in all things important in life. And for my family; none of this would be possible without you. I love you all.

Tawny Lara: I would like to thank my love, Nick, for exploring my body—and mind. My writing would not be possible without the support of our grumpy cat, Meg White and our anxious dog Clara Schumann. I also want to thank my mentor, podcast co-host and close friend Lisa Smith for her patience and guidance.

Christy Leis: Thank you to my Moosh, my Roc and my Mare. And to my Mexican and Filipino family: Gram and Gramps; Gramma Conchita and Grampa Saring; all my relations past, present and future, including the significant male figures and incredibly strong women in my life.

Thank you to Anna David for allowing me to share my story and Ryan Aliapoulios for helping me shape it. Thank you Dr. Gabor Matè for compiling a life-changing and empowering process, Compassionate Inquiry, that gets to the healing and gives inherent dignity back to those who have gone without.

Jessica Lopez: My husband Ricardo Lopez: for your love, laughter, loyalty and unwavering support. For lifting me out of some of the darkest times in my life. For your unselfishness, for putting your family first always and for reminding me that in this life, since I found you, I will never be alone again.

My children Javier and Liliana—my two little miracles...for pushing Mama to be the best person she can be, for giving me the inspiration to heal myself and for being the sole reason I want to change the legacy in our family.

My mother Carla Harwood: for always supporting me; I couldn't have done this without you. For being willing to speak openly and honestly with me about the hard things...for us to both heal in this process.

Larry Varney: for being that father figure I thought I

would never get to experience. For always being a calming voice of reason, and for being the best "Baba" to Javier & Liliana.

Laura Suter: for staying by my side for the last 35 years. Keeping it real with me—riding this roller coaster of life and never judging me. For walking through the hardest times of our lives together and for being the sister that I never had.

Meghan Van Fleet: for our daily 9 am check-ins to keep us stay-at-home moms sane! For laughing and crying with me. For making me never feel alone. For looking back on our high school years and knowing we made it!

Laura Keating: For validating my feelings always. For truly listening to me. For being such a cheerleader in my life, for pushing me to always be a better version of myself and for your undying loyalty during some of the toughest of times in my life. After 20 years apart, I am so blessed to have you back in my life, my soul sister.

Jennifer Lovely: Joe and Jake Lovely, you are my hearts outside my body. You are unconditional love in action; thank you for choosing me as your Mama.

Amy C. Emily, thank you for seeing me, and believing in me.

Shiela Mohn: You showed me that grace was possible, Forever in gratitude.

Daniel Algeo: Thank you for witnessing and holding space and for your compassion, empathy and love. You believed in us.

Dave: Thank you for guiding me along the she-ro's journey; your treasure maps have been full of gold.

Rodney Mueller: Thank you for your strong stand for my life and my wisdom.

Marcia: Thank you for your sarcasm, your play and

your friendship. Thank you to all of those that have walked this path ahead of me that held the light.

Sean Paul Mahoney: Special thanks to Anna David for thinking of me. To inspirations no longer in this realm like Raymond Carver and Carrie Fisher for making me who I am, for my siblings who were the first to laugh at my jokes and for my cat Larry, who snuggles as intensely as he eats.

Jacq Maren: My heart, love and gratitude belong to Jonathan, my *rock*; Tristan, my "Why"; Sarah, my soul's support; Carmen, for bringing the tough love and spiritual awakening; Krista for the trauma work and accountability; Kaitlin and Cara, for sharing this (sometimes crooked!) journey with me. And to my mother, Alicia, I thank you for being my life's greatest teacher against many odds and for proving that it's never too late for forgiveness, healing and love.

Victoria English Martin: Thank you to My Heavenly Father; my father, Robert English; my children, Lauren, Kelly, Daniel and Aubrey; Dr. Dev Paul and my oncology team; my anchor sisters and my pink sisters, as well as Gloriana, Father Tobin, Lolly, Venessa, DWR, Annie Grace/TNMI, Nikki and finally myself...scars and all.

Patrick O'Neil: A grateful thank you to Chris F. and Jason T. I wouldn't be clean and sober without you guys. A heartfelt shout out to everyone at the Monday Night Candlelight meeting in Echo Park and the Bridge Back Topic Discussion in Los Feliz—thank you for all your support. Much love to my wife Jennifer, we do this recovery thing together. I love and miss you Wayne O'Neil, you supported me through all the rough times getting clean and I wish you were still with us.

Emily Lynn Paulson: Thank you to my number one fan club: The other six members of the Paulson seven (Kale, Keegan, Riley, Macy, Lainey, Rowan), Anna David and Launch Pad Pub for the opportunity to contribute to this incredible anthology and The Sober Mom Squad & The Luckiest Club for keeping me sane and sober during the pandemic. Also, my pandemic puppy, Buddy, for keeping my feet warm while I wrote.

Emily Redondo: I'd like to thank God for giving purpose to my train wrecks and courage in my steps; my mother for showing me the way; my husband for giving me room to grow; my children for unconditional love and for recovering alongside me; Ingrid for telling the truth and being hilarious; Anna David for continuously teaching me and believing in me when I don't believe in myself as a writer. And to everyone caught in the middle of what feels like the loneliest place on Earth, I acknowledge you. I write for you.

Paul Roux: Forever grateful to God for what He has done in my life. My parents for their continued love and support on my journey. My dear friends Colin and Alison for sacrificing their time and imparting so much wisdom which I hang on to every day. A big thank you to my friend Richard who has helped me so much. My friends in the Cape Town fellowship who have shown incredible support, love and encouragement over the years. And my family, both local and abroad who I am blessed for having in my life.

Becky Sasso: I'm grateful for all the recovery warriors who share their stories to carry a message of hope to desperate, dying addicts. I would not be alive today if I hadn't heard my own story in the rooms and learned it could have a different ending. Thank you to Rhonda, Jill and Connie for wearing good shoes and Aileen for the years of quiet, steady love. Thanks to my framily, especially my lifelong cosmic soul sister Andi and "my person" Carolyn, my first real friend in LA. I'm forever grateful to Anna, for believing in me and allowing me to make my passion my work. Finally, thanks to my boys—Chris and Charlie. I can't imagine doing this life with anybody else.

Lauren Schwarzfeld: I'm so grateful to the people who've given me the freedom and support to find my way, especially the ones I get to spend every minute with during a pandemic...who knew that would be a thing... the one I married, Karl and our three babes, Mia, Jacob and Abigail. Thank you to my first friend, my forever friend, my sister, Katy. Thank you to the women who have seen me through it all: Kristin and Meghan. To the women who came into my life as an adult and have let me change and become and have encouraged me—you are also the best vacation friends. Thank you Emily Lynn Paulson for modeling what sobriety could be and being an incredible resource to me and this entire community.

Bucky Sinister: I would love to thank all the sober comics who helped me out and talked me down in the hard times and through all the challenges, but most of them would prefer not to be named. So here's to the "normie" comics who helped me find my way: W. Kamau Bell, Al Madrigal, Sean Keane, Chris Garcia, Alex Koll and Caitlin Gill.

The same goes for a lot of actors and entertainment industry people I met in Los Angeles 12-step meetings, from A-listers to YouTube stars. All of you kept my head on straight while I went through the wringer of comparison and professional competition. All those nights hanging out at House of Pies kept me sane. Patty melts, cream pies and late-night coffee are the best medications I could ask for.

Lisa Smith: I want to thank my husband, Craig, for making this California story possible, and my incredible family for always supporting my journey, wherever it leads me.